This book belongs to

....

Date

....

An All-in-One Study
on Living Wisely

proverbs

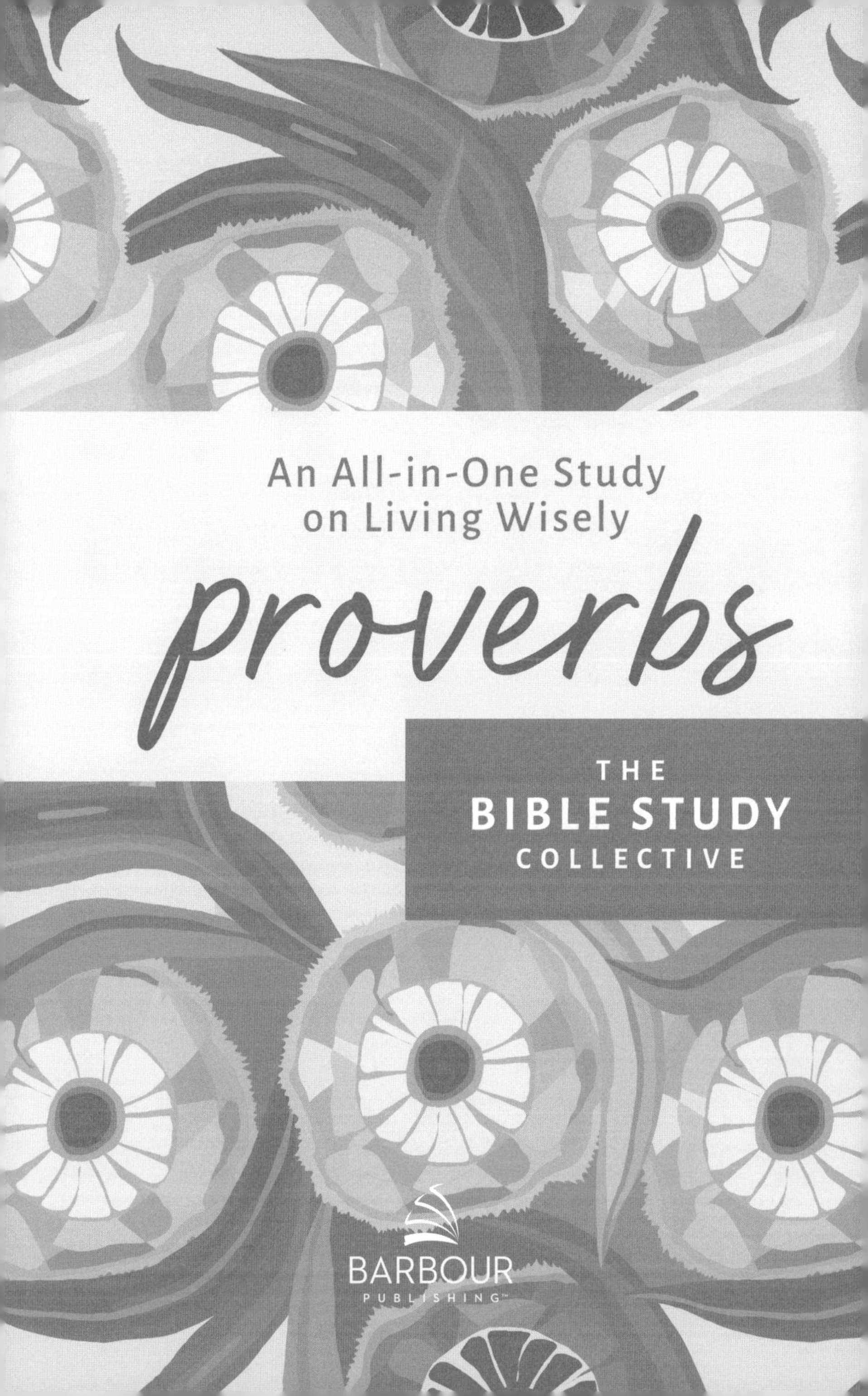
An All-in-One Study
on Living Wisely
proverbs
THE
BIBLE STUDY
COLLECTIVE
BARBOUR
PUBLISHING™

YOU are the reason we do what we do here at Barbour Publishing. We promise that we will always use our God-given talents to produce content with you in mind—and that we will remain biblically faithful, no matter what.

Thank you for being the heart of our business.

Editorial assistance by Melanie Ann Panagiotopoulou.

ISBN 979-8-89151-298-6

Published by Barbour Publishing, Inc., 1810 Barbour Drive, Uhrichsville, Ohio 44683, www.barbourbooks.com

Our mission is to inspire the world with the life-changing message of the Bible.

Printed in China.

Contents

Introduction 9

Study 1: Proverbs 1:1–19 11

Study 2: Proverbs 1:20–33.... 17

Study 3: Proverbs 2:1–22 23

Study 4: Proverbs 3:1–19 29

Study 5: Proverbs 4:1–22 35

Study 6: Proverbs 6:1–19 41

Study 7: Proverbs 7:1–23 47

Study 8: Proverbs 8:10–31.... 53

Study 9: Proverbs 9:1–18 59

Study 10: Proverbs 10:1–17 65

Study 11: Proverbs 11:4–14, 24–31 71

Study 12: Proverbs 12:9–28 77

Study 13: Proverbs 13:4–25 83

Study 14: Proverbs 14:1, 12, 17, 20–35 89

Study 15: Proverbs 15:1–20 95

Study 16: Proverbs 16:3, 8–9, 14–32 101

Study 17: Proverbs 17:1–22 107
Study 18: Proverbs 18:10–24 113
Study 19: Proverbs 20:1–3, 15–30 119
Study 20: Proverbs 21:2–20, 31 125
Study 21: Proverbs 22:1–16 131
Study 22: Proverbs 22:17–29 137
Study 23: Proverbs 23:17–18, 22–25, 29–35 143
Study 24: Proverbs 24:3–4, 13–22, 30–34 149
Study 25: Proverbs 25:1–11, 15, 18–19, 21–22 155
Study 26: Proverbs 27:1–4, 7–10, 17–18, 23–27 161
Study 27: Proverbs 28:1–2, 8–18, 23–25 167
Study 28: Proverbs 29:9–27 173
Study 29: Proverbs 30:1, 3–9, 20–32 179
Study 30: Proverbs 31:1, 10–31 185

THE BIBLE STUDY COLLECTIVE

Welcome to *Proverbs: An All-in-One Study on Living Wisely*—a collection of thirty select proverbs, plus guidance and encouragement for digging into them yourself.

Proverbs is all about wisdom. On one level, wisdom describes skill in living, or practical knowledge. Wise people behave in a way that maximizes blessing for themselves and others in the world that God created.

But on a deeper level, wisdom refers to a proper attitude toward God. It is characterized by "fear." This is not a fright that makes us want to escape something negative. Rather, this fear, a type of awe, is what we should feel when in the presence of the Creator of the universe!

Each study in this guide includes an introduction to the verses from a chapter in Proverbs, followed by the selected verses on the next page. The third through the fifth pages of each study highlight the three steps in what is called the "inductive method" of Bible study: observation, interpretation, and application.

Here's how it works:

- *Observation* answers the question "What does it say?" In other words, what is the actual content in the text?
- *Interpretation* answers the question "What does it mean?" In this step, you'll consider the author's original intent and meaning.
- Finally, *application* answers the questions "What does it mean to you—and how can you apply it to your life?"

Each study in this guide ends with a select verse (or verses) from the chapter you've just studied, as well as related scriptures, for memorization and meditation.

Our prayer is that *Proverbs: An All-in-One Study on Living Wisely* will help you to better understand God's Word and to apply its timeless truth to your own life of faith in the Lord Jesus Christ.

Barbour Publishing

Study 1

PROVERBS 1:1–19

The first nine chapters of the book of Proverbs introduce foundational themes relating to wisdom. The opening verses of Proverbs 1 establish the book's credibility by identifying the author as Solomon, the wisest man ever (1 Kings 3:12) apart from Jesus Christ.

These initial verses of Proverbs emphasize how reverence (or *fear*) of the Lord is the beginning of true knowledge. Wisdom is contrasted with the foolishness of rejecting instruction. Rather than flirting with sin, wise people avoid it entirely. A Christian's goal should never be to see how close she can get to sinning while holding on to her faith. The goal should be to stay off the sinful path altogether.

PROVERBS 1:1–19 OUTLINE

(VERSE 1)	Introduction of author, Solomon
(VERSES 2–4)	Young people should learn wisdom, instruction, knowledge
(VERSES 5–6)	Wise people seek God-centered learning to understand
(VERSE 7)	Fear or awe of the Lord is the beginning of true knowledge
(VERSES 8–9)	Wisdom starts when children heed godly parents
(VERSES 10–14	Avoid any temptation to violence and greed
(VERSES 15–16)	Avoid the sinners' violent pathway
(VERSES 17–19)	Illegal and immoral profit leads to death

Instruction and Exhortation to Sons

[1]The proverbs of Solomon, the son of David, king of Israel:
[2]To know wisdom and instruction; to perceive the words of understanding;
[3]to receive the instruction of wisdom, justice, and judgment, and equity;
[4]to give good judgment to the simple, to the young man knowledge and discretion.
[5]A wise man will hear and will increase learning, and a man of understanding shall attain wise counsels,
[6]to understand a proverb and the interpretation, the words of the wise and their riddles.
[7]The fear of the Lord is the beginning of knowledge, but fools despise wisdom and instruction.
[8]My son, hear the instruction of your father, and do not abandon the law of your mother,
[9]for they shall be an ornament of grace to your head and chains about your neck.
[10]My son, if sinners entice you, do not consent.
[11]If they say, "Come with us; let us lie in wait for blood; let us lurk secretly for the innocent without cause;
[12]let us swallow them up alive like the grave and whole like those who go down to the pit;
[13]we shall find all precious possessions; we shall fill our houses with plunder;
[14]cast in your lot among us; let us all have one purse"—
[15]my son, do not walk in the way with them; refrain your foot from their path,
[16]for their feet run to evil and hurry to shed blood.
[17]Surely the net is spread in vain in the sight of any bird.
[18]And they lie in wait for their own blood; they lurk secretly for their own lives.

[19]So are the ways of everyone who is greedy for gain,
which takes away the life of its owners.

Observe

According to verses 2–4, what is the main purpose of these proverbial sayings?

How does this passage define the relationship between the fear of the Lord and knowledge?

What kind of people will godly wisdom protect you from?

Interpret

What does it mean to "know wisdom and instruction" (verse 2)?

How would you define "the fear the LORD" (verse 7)?

Why does the writer encourage his readers to "hear the instruction" of their fathers and mothers?

How can you show wisdom and understanding in your everyday decision-making?

How would you handle a situation in which friends encouraged you to do something wrong? What would you say to them?

What is one time you avoided a bad choice? What did you learn from it?

Proverbs 1:1–19 Scripture for Memorization/Meditation

The fear of the LORD is the beginning of knowledge,
but fools despise wisdom and instruction.
VERSE 7

Verses for Further Memorization/Meditation

- And the speech pleased the Lord, that Solomon had asked for this thing. And God said to him, "Because you have asked for this thing, and have not asked for yourself long life, nor have asked for riches for yourself, nor have asked for the life of your enemies, but have asked for yourself understanding to discern judgment, behold, I have done according to your words. Behold, I have given you a wise and understanding heart so that there has been none like you before you, nor shall any arise like you after you" (1 Kings 3:10–12).
- "As the thief is ashamed when he is found, so the house of Israel is ashamed—they, their kings, their princes, and their priests, and their prophets" (Jeremiah 2:26).
- I have restrained my feet from every evil way, that I might keep Your word (Psalm 119:101).
- For the love of money is the root of all evil, which while some coveted after, they have gone astray from the faith and pierced themselves through with many sorrows (1Timothy 6:10).

Study 2

PROVERBS 1:20–33

Verse 20 poetically personifies wisdom as a woman. She calls out to the simple, scorners, and fools, urging them to embrace understanding and correction. Despite their resistance, wisdom extends a generous message of mercy to all—if we seek, we will find.

The rejection of wisdom is not the result of ignorance. Because of sin, we human beings make a deliberate choice to follow our own way instead of God's. But that path away from God leads to pain and destruction. Choosing wisdom, though, means security and freedom from fear, the ability to enjoy life as God meant it to be. By heeding Wisdom's call, we can avoid the consequences of foolish disobedience. We can walk in God's protection and peace.

It's up to each and every human being to choose: Will we live life with God or not? There are no excuses for making the wrong decision.

PROVERBS 1:20–33 OUTLINE

(VERSES 20–21):	Wisdom cries out to all
(VERSE 22):	Wisdom wonders why people disregard her
(VERSE 23):	Wisdom offers mercy to those who listen
(VERSES 24–25):	Godly wisdom and counsel is ignored
(VERSES 26–28):	Wisdom will mock unbelievers in their distress
(VERSES 29–32):	Fools reject God, choosing their own way to destruction
(VERSE 33):	Wisdom promises peace and security to those who heed her words

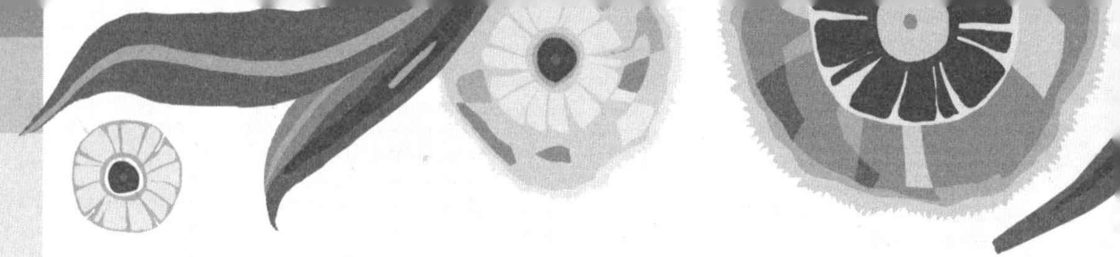

Instruction and Exhortation to Sons

20Wisdom cries outside; she utters her voice in the streets.

21She cries in the chief place of gathering, in the openings of the gates; she utters her words in the city, saying,

22"How long, you simple ones, will you love simplicity, and the scorners delight in their scorning, and fools hate knowledge?

23Turn at my rebuke. Behold, I will pour out my spirit to you; I will make my words known to you.

24Because I have called and you refused, I have stretched out my hand, and no man paid attention.

25But you have neglected all my counsel and would have none of my rebuke.

26I will also laugh at your calamity; I will mock when your fear comes,

27when your fear comes like desolation and your destruction comes like a whirlwind, when distress and anguish come upon you.

28Then they shall call on me, but I will not answer; they shall earnestly seek me, but they shall not find me,

29because they hated knowledge and did not choose the fear of the Lord.

30They would have none of my counsel; they despised all my rebuke.

31Therefore, they shall eat of the fruit of their own way and be filled with their own devices.

32For the turning away of the simple shall slay them, and the prosperity of fools shall destroy them.

33But whoever listens to me shall dwell safely and shall be at peace without fear of evil."

Observe

How is wisdom portrayed in this passage?

What direct quotes are attributed to wisdom? To whom are they addressed?

What promise is made to the people who listen to wisdom?

Interpret

Why would God instruct Solomon to identify wisdom as a woman?

What does the statement, "Behold, I will pour out my spirit to you; I will make my words known to you" (verse 23) mean?

What emotions do verses 23 and 33 evoke? Why?

Apply

How can you be ready to hear Wisdom's rebuke?

What specific choices can you make in order to "dwell safely and. . .be at peace" (verse 33)?

How can you best respond when others around you are ignoring God and His wisdom?

Proverbs 1:20–33 Scripture for Memorization/Meditation

"Turn at my rebuke. Behold, I will pour out my spirit to you; I will make my words known to you."
VERSE 23

Verses for Further Memorization/Meditation

- "And it shall come to pass afterward that I will pour out My Spirit on all flesh, and your sons and your daughters shall prophesy, your old men shall dream dreams, your young men shall see visions" (Joel 2:28).
- But My people would not listen to My voice, and Israel would have none of Me (Psalm 81:11).
- On the last day, that great day of the feast, Jesus stood and cried, saying, "If any man thirsts, let him come to Me and drink" (John 7:37).
- But to those who are called, both Jews and Greeks, Christ the power of God and the wisdom of God (1 Corinthians 1:24).
- But of Him you are in Christ Jesus, who from God was made for us wisdom, and righteousness and sanctification and redemption (1 Corinthians 1:30).
- That their hearts might be comforted, being knit together in love, and to all riches of the full assurance of understanding, to the acknowledgment of the mystery of God, and of the Father, and of Christ, in whom are hidden all the treasures of wisdom and knowledge (Colossians 2:2–3).

Study 3

PROVERBS 2:1–22

According to Proverbs 2, godly wisdom is one of life's greatest treasures, offering guidance and protection to those who seek it. It keeps us from falling in with the wrong crowd.

Wisdom also protects against sexual immorality. But this is not an avoidance of all sexual activity; rather, Proverbs warns of illicit behavior. Proverbs 5 celebrates the physical pleasures of marriage.

Most of all, pursuing God's wisdom leads to a life that pleases Him—and isn't that what life is all about? Blessings, regardless of our circumstances, will follow.

Proverbs 2:1–22 Outline

(VERSES 1–4)	Choices for upright living
(VERSE 5)	The reward of seeking godly wisdom
(VERSE 6)	Wisdom, knowledge, and understanding come from God
(VERSES 7–9)	God grants wisdom, protection, and guidance
(VERSE 10)	Wisdom is pleasant to the soul
(VERSE 11)	Understanding protects a person
(VERSES 12–15)	Wisdom protects from bad company
(VERSES 16–19)	Wisdom protects from sexual immorality
(VERSES 20–21)	The wise please God
(VERSE 22)	The unwise will be separated from God and suffer

To Sons, Continued

[1]My son, if you will receive my words and hide my commandments with you,

[2]so that you incline your ear to wisdom and apply your
heart to understanding—

[3]yes, if you cry after knowledge and lift up your voice for
understanding,

[4]if you seek her as silver and search for her as for hidden
treasures—

[5]then you shall understand the fear of the Lord and find
the knowledge of God.

[6]For the Lord gives wisdom; out of His mouth comes knowledge and understanding.

[7]He lays up sound wisdom for the righteous; He is a shield
to those who walk uprightly.

[8]He keeps the paths of judgment and preserves the way
of His saints.

[9]Then you shall understand righteousness and judgment
and equity—yes, every good path.

[10]When wisdom enters into your heart and knowledge is
pleasant to your soul,

[11]discretion shall preserve you; understanding shall keep
you,

[12]to deliver you from the way of the evil man, from the
man who speaks perverse things,

[13]from those who leave the paths of uprightness to walk
in the ways of darkness,

[14]who rejoice to do evil and delight in the perversity of
the wicked,

[15]whose ways are crooked, and they are perverse in their
paths;

[16]to deliver you from the strange woman, from the stranger
who flatters with her words,

17who forsakes the guide of her youth and forgets the
covenant of her God.
18For her house inclines to death, and her paths to the dead.
19None who go to her return again, nor do they take hold
of the paths of life.
20So you will walk in the way of good men and keep the
paths of the righteous.
21For the upright shall dwell in the land, and the perfect
shall remain in it.
22But the wicked shall be cut off from the earth, and the
transgressors shall be uprooted from it.

Observe

What is the source of all wisdom? What does wisdom accomplish in human lives?

....

....

....

....

How does Solomon encourage his readers to seek after wisdom (verses 3–4)?

....

....

....

....

....

What does the final verse say of those who do not choose wisdom?

Interpret

Why does God offer His wisdom to human beings? What is He hoping to accomplish by that?

How would pursuing God's wisdom protect a person from "the man who speaks perverse things" (verse 12)?

Do you think Solomon's warnings against a "strange [or immoral] woman" (verse 16) are limited only to females? Why or why not?

What specific actions can you take to "cry after knowledge" and "seek her as silver" (verses 3–4)?

Who in your life—whether actual acquaintances or online influences—tries to lead you astray from God? What can you do about that?

If you ever get off "the paths of the righteous" (verse 20), how can you return to God?

Proverbs 2:1–22 Scripture for Memorization/Meditation

For the Lord gives wisdom; out of His mouth
comes knowledge and understanding.
VERSE 6

Verses for Further Memorization/Meditation

- He will watch over the feet of His saints, and the wicked shall be silent in darkness, for no man shall prevail by strength (1 Samuel 2:9).
- "And this is the condemnation, that light has come into the world, and men loved darkness rather than light, because their deeds were evil" (John 3:19).
- "Therefore whoever hears these sayings of Mine and does them, I will compare him to a wise man who built his house on a rock. And the rain descended, and the floods came, and the winds blew and beat on that house, and it did not fall, for it was founded on a rock" (Matthew 7:24–25).
- And even as they did not like to retain God in their knowledge, God gave them over to a reprobate mind, to do those things that are not proper (Romans 1:28).
- If any of you lacks wisdom, let him ask of God, who gives to all men generously and without reproach, and it shall be given him (James 1:5).

Study 4

PROVERBS 3:1–19

Verses from Proverbs 3 are some of the most often quoted from Solomon's teaching. Among other things, this chapter describes how young people should heed their parents' wisdom to avoid the pain that foolish living inevitably brings.

Wisdom's value is compared to precious metals and jewels. When we make wisdom part of our lives, we gain length of life, riches and honor, pleasantness, and peace. Rejecting wisdom actually contradicts the very structure of creation itself!

Proverbs 3:1–19 Outline

(VERSES 1–2)	Obey your parents' wisdom
(VERSES 3–4)	Holding on to mercy and truth leads to God's favor
(VERSE 5)	Wisdom comes from a God-focused heart
(VERSE 6)	Following God's will leads you on the right path
(VERSE 7–8)	Trusting God and avoiding evil makes for physical well-being
(VERSES 9–10)	Giving to God shows trust, and His blessings follow
(VERSES 11–12)	God's discipline corrects and improves His children
(VERSES 13–18)	Wisdom brings happiness, wealth, peace, and life
(VERSE 19)	God created the heavens and earth by wisdom

To Sons, Continued

1My son, do not forget my law, but let your heart keep my commandments.

2For they shall add to you length of days and long life and peace.

3Do not let mercy and truth forsake you; bind them around your neck; write them on the tablet of your heart,

4so you shall find favor and good understanding in the sight of God and man.

5Trust in the Lord with all your heart and do not lean on your own understanding.

6In all your ways acknowledge Him, and He shall direct your paths.

7Do not be wise in your own eyes; fear the Lord and depart from evil.

8It shall be health to your navel and marrow to your bones.

9Honor the Lord with your possessions and with the first-fruits of all your increase,

10so your barns shall be filled with plenty and your presses shall burst with new wine.

11My son, do not despise the discipline of the Lord or be weary of His correction.

12For those whom the Lord loves, He corrects, like a father with the son in whom he delights.

13Happy is the man who finds wisdom and the man who gets understanding,

14for its profit is better than the profit of silver, and its gain than fine gold.

15She is more precious than rubies, and all the things you can desire are not to be compared to her.

16Length of days is in her right hand, and in her left hand riches and honor.

17Her ways are ways of pleasantness, and all her paths are peace.

[18]She is a tree of life to those who lay hold of her, and happy is everyone who retains her.
[19]The LORD, by wisdom, has founded the earth; by understanding He has established the heavens.

Observe

What specific benefits come to a believer who wisely trusts in the Lord?

How does wisdom compare to the valuable things of this world (verses 13–15)?

What do the Lord's discipline and correction accomplish in our lives?

Interpret

What do the twin commands of verse 1—"do not forget my law" and "keep my commandments"—look like in real life?

Why is trusting the Lord more reliable than relying on our own understanding?

Do you think the promise of "length of days and long life" (verse 2) is a guarantee in this world? Why or why not?

How can you "bind" mercy and truth "around your neck" and "write them on the tablet of your heart" (verse 3)?

How can you respond positively to God's discipline in your life?

What should you do when you suffer from ill health or financial difficulties or some other negative experience?

Proverbs 3:1–19 Scriptures for Memorization/Meditation

My son, do not forget my law, but let your heart keep my commandments. For they shall add to you length of days and long life and peace.
VERSES 1–2

Trust in the LORD with all your heart and do not lean on your own understanding. In all your ways acknowledge Him, and He shall direct your paths.
VERSES 5–6

Verses for Further Memorization/Meditation

- And out of the ground the LORD God made to grow every tree that is pleasant to the sight and good for food. The tree of life was also in the midst of the garden, and the tree of knowledge of good and evil (Genesis 2:9).
- "And you, Solomon, my son, know the God of your father, and serve Him with a perfect heart and with a willing mind, for the LORD searches all hearts and understands all the intentions of the thoughts. If you seek Him, He will be found by you, but if you forsake Him, He will cast you off forever" (1 Chronicles 28:9).
- Those who love Your law have great peace, and nothing shall offend them (Psalm 119:165).
- And you have forgotten the exhortation that speaks to you as to children, "My son, do not despise the chastening of the Lord or be discouraged when you are rebuked by Him, for whom the Lord loves He chastens, and He scourges every son whom He receives" (Hebrews 12:5–6).

Study 5

PROVERBS 4:1–22

These verses emphasize how loving parents are a child's best teachers. The home is where the young should learn right from wrong.

Solomon reflects on the life lessons of his father, David, who was not only his king but also his spiritual guide. David, a man after God's own heart (1 Samuel 13:14), encouraged Solomon to follow God's commands, emphasizing the importance of wisdom in the boy's life. This is likely why Solomon, when given the chance to ask God for anything, chose wisdom (1 Kings 3:9; 2 Chronicles 1:7–10).

We today, living after the life, death, and resurrection of Jesus Christ, can understand more fully how God's wisdom benefits us both now and for eternity.

Proverbs 4:1–22 Outline

(VERSES 1–4)	Home should be wisdom's foundation
(VERSES 5–6)	Value wisdom and it will protect you
(VERSE 7)	Wisdom is life's greatest treasure
(VERSES 8–9)	Wisdom brings honor and glory
(VERSE 10)	Heeding wisdom leads to long life
(VERSES 11–13)	Follow instruction to avoid obstacles and achieve success
(VERSES 14–17)	Avoid wickedness and its bad consequences
(VERSES 18–19)	The path of the just is compared to the sad way of the wicked
(VERSES 20–22)	Listening to God's wisdom brings life and health

To Sons, Continued

1Hear, you children, the instruction of a father, and attend to
know understanding.
2For I give you good doctrine; do not forsake my law.
3For I was my father's son, tender and only beloved in the
sight of my mother.
4He also taught me and said to me, "Let your heart retain
my words; keep my commandments and live.
5Get wisdom. Get understanding. Do not forget it or turn
away from the words of my mouth.
6Do not forsake her, and she shall preserve you. Love her,
and she shall keep you.
7Wisdom is the principal thing. Therefore, get wisdom,
and with all your getting, get understanding.
8Exalt her, and she shall promote you; she shall bring you
to honor when you embrace her.
9She shall give to your head an ornament of grace; she
shall deliver to you a crown of glory."
10Hear, O my son, and receive my sayings, and the years
of your life shall be many.
11I have taught you in the way of wisdom; I have led you
in right paths.
12When you go, your steps shall not be hindered, and when
you run, you shall not stumble.
13Take firm hold of instruction; do not let her go. Keep
her, for she is your life.
14Do not enter into the path of the wicked, and do not go
in the way of evil men.
15Avoid it; do not pass by it; turn from it and pass away.
16For they do not sleep, unless they have done evil, and
their sleep is taken away, unless they cause some to fall.
17For they eat the bread of wickedness and drink the wine
of violence.
18But the path of the just is like the shining light that shines

more and more until the perfect day.
19The way of the wicked is like darkness; they do not know
what they stumble over.
20My son, attend to my words; incline your ear to my
sayings.
21Do not let them depart from your eyes; keep them in
the midst of your heart.
22For they are life to those who find them and health to
all their flesh.

Observe

What key words describe how Solomon's father, David, felt about wisdom?

....

....

....

....

....

How do Solomon's own words to his son (verses 10–22) compare and contrast with David's teaching to Solomon (verses 4–9)?

....

....

....

....

....

How is the way of evil men described? How is the way of the just?

Interpret

What did King David mean by "with all your getting, get understanding" (verse 7)?

What impact did David's words seem to have on his son Solomon? Does a parent's good teaching guarantee that the child will succeed? Why or why not?

How do wicked people's actions show their separation from wisdom?

How passionately do you seek wisdom in your daily decisions? Could you do better?

Why might a person "forget" wisdom (verse 5)? How can you avoid that?

How can you help a younger person avoid falling in with the wrong crowd?

Proverbs 4:1–22 Scripture for Memorization/Meditation

My son, attend to my words; incline your ear to my sayings. Do not let them depart from your eyes; keep them in the midst of your heart. For they are life to those who find them and health to all their flesh.
VERSES 20–22

Verses for Further Memorization/Meditation

- "Therefore give Your servant an understanding heart to judge Your people, that I may discern between good and bad. For who is able to judge this great people of Yours?" (1 Kings 3:9).
- "Therefore the Lord God of Israel says, 'I said indeed that your house and the house of your father should walk before Me forever.' But now the Lord says, 'Far be it from Me, for those who honor Me I will honor, and those who despise Me shall be lightly regarded" (1 Samuel 2:30).
- Blessed is the man who does not walk in the counsel of the ungodly or stand in the way of sinners or sit in the seat of the scornful (Psalm 1:1).
- "That you may be the children of your Father who is in heaven. For He makes His sun to rise on the evil and on the good, and sends rain on the just and on the unjust" (Matthew 5:45).

Study 6

PROVERBS 6:1–19

This chapter of Proverbs begins with a firm warning against making monetary promises for others. This can be a destructive trap, so people caught in such situations must act fast to escape.

Relating to the topic of money, laziness is roundly criticized. The hardworking ant is held up as an example to lazy people, who desire too much rest and sleep. That leads to poverty, which can creep up on a person very quickly.

Deceitful people—scoundrels or hucksters—pretend to be friends but exploit others for personal gain. Their lifestyle is one to beware of and is something that God will not bless.

Proverbs 6 then lists seven things God hates, beginning with pride, dishonesty, and violence. These traits are described from head to foot, showing how sin corrupts a person entirely. The last two traits focus on corrupt leaders who use lies and division for power. God despises these behaviors and will bring judgment on those who practice them.

PROVERBS 6:1–19 OUTLINE

(VERSES 1–5)	Avoid being a guarantor
(VERSES 6–11)	Be as industrious as an ant
(VERSES 12–14)	Beware of scoundrels
(VERSE 15)	Scoundrels will not be blessed
(VERSES 16–18)	Seven things God hates

To Sons, Continued

1My son, if you become surety for your friend, if you have shaken your hand with a stranger,

2you are snared with the words of your mouth; you are taken with the words of your mouth.

3Do this now, my son, and deliver yourself when you have come into the hand of your friend: go, humble yourself, and plead with your friend.

4Do not give sleep to your eyes or slumber to your eyelids.

5Deliver yourself like a gazelle from the hand of the hunter and like a bird from the hand of the fowler.

6Go to the ant, you sluggard! Consider her ways and be wise,

7which, having no guide, overseer, or ruler,

8provides her food in the summer and gathers her food in the harvest.

9How long will you sleep, O sluggard? When will you arise from your sleep?

10Yet a little sleep, a little slumber, a little folding of the hands to sleep,

11so your poverty shall come like one who travels and your need like an armed man.

12An evil person, a wicked man, walks with a perverse mouth.

13He winks with his eyes; he speaks with his feet; he teaches with his fingers.

14Perversity is in his heart; he devises evil continually; he sows discord.

15Therefore, his calamity shall come suddenly; suddenly he shall be broken without remedy.

16These six things the Lord hates—yes, seven are an abomination to Him:

17a proud look, a lying tongue, and hands that shed innocent blood,

[18]a heart that devises wicked plans, feet that are swift in running to evil,
[19]a false witness who speaks lies, and he who sows discord among brothers.

Observe

How does this passage show the danger of careless words? What does it suggest for dealing with foolish promises?

What does King Solomon have to say about lazy people? What is his suggestion for "sluggards"?

What are the seven things God hates? How do the final two differ from the first five?

Interpret

Why are verses 1–5 so adamant about staying out of financial entanglements? What does the imagery of verse 5 say about the issue?

Among all the animals, why is the ant chosen as an example of industry? What can human beings learn from the ant's good qualities?

Why would God choose the seven specific "abominations" of verses 16–19? What do they reveal about His character and values?

What financial practices or attitudes in your life might need to be revisited? How can you make changes to benefit yourself and your family?

....

....

....

....

....

How hard of a worker would you say you are? Are there any areas of your life in which you could use your time and energies better?

....

....

....

....

....

When have you personally struggled with any of the seven things God hates? What steps can you take to make positive changes in your life?

....

....

....

....

....

Proverbs 6:1–19 Scriptures for Memorization/Meditation

Go to the ant, you sluggard!
Consider her ways and be wise.
VERSE 6

Yet a little sleep, a little slumber, a little folding of the hands to sleep, so your poverty shall come like one who travels and your need like an armed man.
VERSES 10–11

Verses for Further Memorization/Meditation

- And God saw that the wickedness of man was great in the earth and that every imagination of the thoughts of his heart was only evil continually. And it grieved the Lord that He had made man on the earth, and it grieved Him in His heart (Genesis 6:5–6).
- "If there is a poor man among you, one of your brothers, within any of your gates in your land that the Lord your God is giving you, you shall not harden your heart or shut your hand from your poor brother, but you shall open your hand wide to him and shall surely lend him sufficient for his need, in what he wants" (Deuteronomy 15:7–8).
- "Give to him who asks you, and do not turn away from him who would borrow from you" (Matthew 5:42).
- Therefore He says, "Awake you who sleep, and arise from the dead, and Christ shall give you light." See then that you walk carefully, not as fools, but as wise, redeeming the time because the days are evil (Ephesians 5:14–16).

Study 7

PROVERBS 7:1–23

Proverbs 7 presents a father's loving and urgent warning to his son to make wise choices. The father emphasizes the need to follow his instruction as if it were a law.

To make his point, the father recounts a scene he witnessed from his own window: A young man walked toward the house of an immoral woman at dusk. She was loud and flirtatious, and sweet-talked the young man into spending the night with her. Promising excitement and pleasure, this woman knew that many young men wouldn't refuse the offer. As expected, this one didn't.

But the wise father warned that yielding to such temptations leads to terrible outcomes. He compared the passive young man to an ox heading to slaughter. The young man was dim-witted, like a bird entering a trap. In the end, such sinful decisions could cost him everything—even his life.

Proverbs 7:1–23 Outline

(VERSES 1–3)	Young people should listen to godly parents
(VERSES 4–5)	Wisdom is like a beloved, wise sister
(VERSES 6–13)	Case study of a foolish young man's sinful path
(VERSES 14–18)	The temptation of forbidden pleasure
(VERSES 19–20)	Deception and marital betrayal
(VERSES 21–23)	Lack of wisdom brings ruin

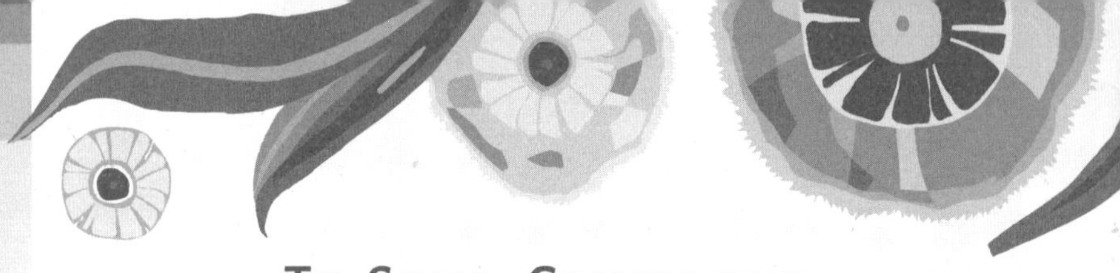

To Sons, Concluded

1My son, keep my words and lay up my commandments with you.

2Keep my commandments and live, and my law as the apple of your eye.

3Bind them on your fingers; write them on the tablet of your heart.

4Say to wisdom, "You are my sister," and call understanding your relative,

5that they may keep you from the adulterous woman, from the immoral woman who flatters with her words.

6For at the window of my house, I looked through my casement

7and saw among the simple ones—I discerned among the youths—a young man void of understanding,

8passing through the street near her corner, and he went the way to her house,

9in the twilight, in the evening, in the black and dark night.

10And, behold, there a woman met him with the attire of a harlot and crafty of heart.

11(She is loud and stubborn; her feet do not remain in her house.

12Now she is outside, now in the streets, and lies in wait at every corner.)

13So she caught him and kissed him and, with an impudent face, said to him,

14"I have peace offerings with me. This day I have paid my vows.

15Therefore, I came out to meet you, to diligently seek your face, and I have found you.

16I have decked my bed with coverings of tapestry, with carved works, with fine linen of Egypt.

17I have perfumed my bed with myrrh, aloes, and cinnamon.

[18]Come, let us take our fill of love until the morning. Let
us solace ourselves with loves.
[19]For my husband is not at home; he has gone on a long
journey.
[20]He has taken a bag of money with him and will come
home on the appointed day."
[21]With her very fair speech she caused him to yield; with
the flattering of her lips she forced him.
[22]He goes after her immediately, like an ox goes to the
slaughter or like a fool to the correction of the stocks,
[23]until a dart strikes through his liver. As a bird hastens
to the snare, he does not know that it is for his life.

Observe

How does the father tell his son to heed his words and commandments?

....

....

....

....

What adjectives describe the adulterous woman of Proverbs 7? What descriptions are given of her young male victim?

....

....

....

....

According to this passage, what happens to a young man (or any person) who yields to sexual temptation?

Interpret

What is the writer suggesting when he urges his son to keep his law "as the apple of your eye" (verse 2)?

What other vices might the adulteress of this passage represent? From biblical example or personal observation, what do you see enticing people to stray from wisdom and moral integrity?

Why are lies and smooth speech so often a part of sinful enticements?

....

....

....

....

Apply

When have the smooth but dishonest words of sinful people threatened to derail you?

....

....

....

....

How might this passage influence which television shows, movies, books, music, or games you consume?

....

....

....

....

What steps can you take to strengthen your moral integrity and fend off the temptations of this world?

....

....

....

....

Proverbs 7:1–23 Scriptures for Memorization/Meditation

Keep my commandments and live,
and my law as the apple of your eye.
VERSE 2

With her very fair speech she caused him to yield;
with the flattering of her lips she forced him.
VERSE 21

Verses for Further Memorization/Meditation

- For man also does not know his time. Like the fish that are taken in an evil net, and like the birds that are caught in a snare, so are the sons of men snared in an evil time when it suddenly falls on them (Ecclesiastes 9:12).
- Flee fornication. Every sin that a man does is outside the body, but he who commits fornication sins against his own body (1 Corinthians 6:18).
- Let the word of Christ dwell in you richly in all wisdom, teaching and admonishing one another in psalms and hymns and spiritual songs, singing with grace in your hearts to the Lord (Colossians 3:16).
- But every man is tempted when he is drawn away by his own lust and enticed. Then when lust has conceived, it brings forth sin. And sin, when it is finished, brings forth death (James 1:14–15).

Study 8

PROVERBS 8:10–31

Wisdom is valued above all material wealth. God's Word describes it as "better than rubies" (Proverbs 8:11).

Though wisdom is accessible to all, its abundance does not reduce its value as the world's system of supply and demand might indicate. Coming as it does from God, wisdom is the deepest and most profound principle. Along with prudence, knowledge, and discretion, wisdom guides believers in living balanced lives.

Wisdom claims to be the first principle of creation. Proverbs 8 emphasizes its status as the oldest guiding force, something of greater value than creation itself. Wisdom finds joy in the world's development, as all creation aligns with its logic. It is an artisan whose truths are woven into the very fabric of the universe.

To truly understand our world, we need the holy wisdom of God. And He is perfectly willing to share it (James 1:5).

PROVERBS 8:10–31 OUTLINE

(VERSES 10–11)	Wisdom excels earthly riches
(VERSE 12)	Wisdom brings prudence and discernment
(VERSE 13)	Wisdom hates evil and pride
(VERSES 14–16)	Wisdom guides leaders and governments
(VERSES 17–21)	Wisdom rewards those who seek her
(VERSES 22–26)	Wisdom's origins
(VERSES 27–29)	Wisdom's part in creation
(VERSES 30–31)	The joy of wisdom

In Praise of Wisdom

10Receive my instruction, and not silver, and knowledge rather than choice gold.

11For wisdom is better than rubies, and all the things that may be desired cannot be compared to it.

12I, wisdom, dwell with prudence and find out knowledge of witty schemes.

13The fear of the LORD is to hate evil; I hate pride and arrogance and the evil way and the perverse mouth.

14Counsel is mine, and sound wisdom; I am understanding; I have strength.

15By me, kings reign and princes decree justice.

16By me, princes rule, and nobles, even all the judges of the earth.

17I love those who love me, and those who earnestly seek me find me.

18Riches and honor are with me—yes, durable riches and righteousness.

19My fruit is better than gold—yes, than fine gold—and my revenue than choice silver.

20I lead in the way of righteousness, in the midst of the paths of judgment,

21that I may cause those who love me to inherit wealth, and I will fill their treasures.

22The LORD possessed me in the beginning of His way, before His works of old.

23I was set up from everlasting, from the beginning, before the earth ever was.

24When there were no depths, I was brought forth, when there were no fountains abounding with water.

25Before the mountains were settled, before the hills, I was brought forth,

26while as yet He had not made the earth or the fields or

the highest part of the dust of the world.
27When He prepared the heavens, I was there. When He
set a circle on the face of the depth,
28when He established the clouds above, when He strengthened the fountains of the deep,
29when He gave His decree to the sea that the waters
should not trespass His commandment, when He appointed
the foundations of the earth,
30then I was beside Him, as one brought up with Him, and
I was His daily delight, rejoicing always before Him,
31rejoicing in the habitable part of His earth. And my
delights were with the sons of men.

Observe

What does wisdom "say" in this chapter?

....

....

....

....

....

How does wisdom describe its relationship with the Lord?

....

....

....

....

....

How does wisdom express joy in the creation process?

Interpret

Why would Solomon personify wisdom by having it speak on its own?

What does wisdom mean when it says, "My fruit is better than gold" (verse 19)?

What does wisdom teach us about our life choices?

Apply

How can you ensure that wisdom is better than silver, gold, and rubies in your own life?

How will a true understanding of the value of wisdom influence your goals and ambitions?

In what ways can you share the benefits of wisdom with others in your life?

Proverbs 8:10–31 Scriptures for Memorization/Meditation

For wisdom is better than rubies, and all the things that may be desired cannot be compared to it.
VERSE 11

When He prepared the heavens, I was there. When He set a circle on the face of the depth, when He established the clouds above, when He strengthened the fountains of the deep, when He gave His decree to the sea that the waters should not trespass His commandment, when He appointed the foundations of the earth, then I was beside Him, as one brought up with Him, and I was His daily delight, rejoicing always before Him, rejoicing in the habitable part of His earth. And my delights were with the sons of men.
VERSES 27–31

Verses for Further Memorization/Meditation

- For God gives wisdom, and knowledge, and joy to a man who is good in His sight. But to the sinner He gives the task of gathering and heaping up, that he may give to him who is good before God (Ecclesiastes 2:26).
- In the beginning was the Word, and the Word was with God, and the Word was God. The same was in the beginning with God. All things were made by Him, and without Him nothing was made that was made (John 1:1–3).
- But to those who are called, both Jews and Greeks, Christ the power of God and the wisdom of God (1 Corinthians 1:24).

Study 9

PROVERBS 9:1–18

Proverbs 9 serves as the conclusion to Solomon's heartfelt appeal to his son. The chapter reinforces the contrast between wisdom and folly.

Wisdom is portrayed as a gracious woman inviting all to her feast. The promise of life and the statement of individual responsibility are a fitting conclusion to the call of wisdom. Her joy and blessings are freely available to those who choose her. Yet for those who reject this message, they will bear the consequences of their foolishness alone.

In contrast, folly is again depicted as a seductive and deceitful woman. She entices the simple into her house, leading to their ruin.

This passages encapsulates the central message of the first nine chapters of Proverbs—wisdom leads to life, while folly brings destruction—before transitioning into the short, practical sayings that begin in Proverbs 10.

Proverbs 9:1–18 Outline

(VERSE 1)	Wisdom is a house built on seven pillars
(VERSE 2)	Wisdom's feast of abundance and joy
(VERSES 3–6)	Wisdom's invitation to all
(VERSES 7–9)	Varying responses to correction
(VERSES 10–11)	The foundation and reward of true wisdom
(VERSE 12)	Individual responsibility to wisdom's call
(VERSES 13–15)	Folly's invitation to the simple
(VERSES 16–18)	Folly's deception

The Praise of Wisdom, Continued

1Wisdom has built her house; she has carved out her seven pillars.

2She has killed her beasts; she has mixed her wine; she has also furnished her table.

3She has sent out her maidens; she cries in the highest places of the city,

4"Whoever is simple, let him turn in here." As for him who lacks understanding, she says to him,

5"Come, eat of my bread and drink of the wine that I have mixed.

6Forsake the foolish and live, and go in the way of understanding."

7He who rebukes a scorner gets shame for himself, and he who rebukes a wicked man gets himself a stain.

8Do not rebuke a scorner, lest he hate you; rebuke a wise man, and he will love you.

9Give instruction to a wise man, and he will be wiser yet; teach a just man, and he will increase in learning.

10The fear of the Lord is the beginning of wisdom, and the knowledge of the holy is understanding.

11For by me your days shall be multiplied and the years of your life shall be increased.

12If you are wise, you shall be wise for yourself, but if you scorn, you shall bear it alone.

13A foolish woman is clamorous; she is simple and knows nothing.

14For she sits at the door of her house, on a seat in the high places of the city,

15to call passengers who go right on their ways,

16"Whoever is simple, let him turn in here." And as for him who lacks understanding, she says to him,

[17]"Stolen waters are sweet, and bread eaten in secret is
pleasant."
[18]But he does not know that the dead are there and that
her guests are in the depths of hell.

Observe

What does Wisdom do and say in this passage?

What does Wisdom offer to those who accept her invitation?

How does a wise man respond to instruction compared to a scorner?

Interpret

Why would Wisdom use the imagery of a feast for inviting the simple?

What do the wise man and the scorner's differing responses to correction reveal about their character? What do these responses say about their relationship to God?

What does the phrase "stolen waters are sweet" (verse 17) suggest about the deceptive appeal of folly?

Apply

In what specific ways can you actively seek and respond to God's call to be wise?

....

....

....

....

....

....

At what times has God's wisdom brought success to your life? How can that experience guide you now?

....

....

....

....

....

....

What practical steps can you take to recognize and avoid the deceptive attractions of folly?

....

....

....

....

....

Proverbs 9:1–18 Scriptures for Memorization/Meditation

The fear of the Lord is the beginning of wisdom,
and the knowledge of the holy is understanding.
VERSE 10

For by me your days shall be multiplied and
the years of your life shall be increased.
VERSE 11

Verses for Further Memorization/Meditation

- And to man He said, "Behold, the fear of the Lord—that is wisdom. And to depart from evil is understanding" (Job 28:28).
- And the Spirit of the Lord shall rest on Him, the Spirit of wisdom and understanding, the Spirit of counsel and might, the Spirit of knowledge and of the fear of the Lord (Isaiah 11:2).
- Now no chastening seems to be joyous for the present, but grievous; nevertheless, afterward it yields the peaceful fruit of righteousness to those who are exercised by it (Hebrews 12:11).
- "For whoever has, to him shall be given, and he shall have abundance. But whoever does not have, even what he has shall be taken away from him" (Matthew 13:12).
- But the wisdom that is from above is first pure, then peaceable, gentle, and easy to reason with; full of mercy and good fruits, without partiality, and without hypocrisy (James 3:17).

Study 10

PROVERBS 10:1–17

In Chapter 10, the book of Proverbs shifts from broader themes to concise, practical sayings that illustrate how wisdom applies to everyday life. These verses often highlight the impact of our choices and actions.

The chapter begins with a timeless observation of how children's behavior affects their parents' happiness. Simply put: Wise children bring joy while foolish ones cause grief. As children grow, hard work on their part gains praise and brings honor to their parents. But laziness in a child results in the parents' shame and sadness.

Proverbs 10 highlights the contrast between two paths—of wealth gained through wrong actions and of success earned through righteousness. The first leads to emptiness, but the second brings lasting blessing. This chapter returns to themes seen earlier in Proverbs: namely, that wise people are open to correction, while unwise people, who need correction the most, reject it.

Proverbs 10:1–17 Outline

(VERSES 1–2)	Wise children bring joy to their parents
(VERSES 3–4)	God provides for the diligent
(VERSE 5)	Diligence versus laziness in a young person
(VERSES 6–11)	Six contrasts of the righteous and the wicked
(VERSES 12–17)	Real-life results of righteousness compared to unrighteousness

The Folly of Wickedness, The Wisdom of Righteousness

1The proverbs of Solomon: A wise son makes a glad father, but a foolish son is the heaviness of his mother.

2Treasures of wickedness profit nothing, but righteousness delivers from death.

3The LORD will not allow the soul of the righteous to famish, but He casts away the substance of the wicked.

4He who deals with a slack hand becomes poor, but the hand of the diligent makes rich.

5He who gathers in summer is a wise son, but he who sleeps in harvest is a son who causes shame.

6Blessings are on the head of the just, but violence covers the mouth of the wicked.

7The memory of the just is blessed, but the name of the wicked shall rot.

8The wise in heart will receive commandments, but a talking fool shall fall.

9He who walks uprightly walks surely, but he who perverts his ways shall be known.

10He who winks with the eye causes sorrow, but a chattering fool shall fall.

11The mouth of a righteous man is a well of life, but violence covers the mouth of the wicked.

12Hatred stirs up strife, but love covers all sins.

13Wisdom is found on the lips of him who has understanding, but a rod is for the back of him who is void of understanding.

14Wise men lay up knowledge, but the mouth of the foolish is near destruction.

15The rich man's wealth is his strong city; the destruction of the poor is their poverty.

[16]The labor of the righteous tends to life, the fruit of the wicked to sin.

[17]He who keeps instruction is in the way of life, but he who refuses correction goes astray.

Observe

According to this passage, how do righteousness and wickedness affect a person's life?

....

....

....

....

What do these verses say about hard work and how it impacts others?

....

....

....

....

How do the actions of the righteous and unrighteous compare?

....

....

....

....

Interpret

Why would Solomon put so much focus on the effect of children's choices upon their parents?

What do you think verse 10 means? Why would Solomon include the pair of negatives within a section of verses showing a positive/negative contrast?

How do wealth and poverty relate to wisdom and righteousness?

Apply

How did your childhood attitudes and actions affect your parents? How can you build off your good choices or deal with your bad ones now?

What steps can you take to embrace correction and instruction from wise believers?

How can you "lay up knowledge" (verse 14)? How can you share such knowledge with others?

Proverbs 10:1–17 Scriptures for Memorization/Meditation

A wise son makes a glad father, but a foolish
son is the heaviness of his mother.
VERSE 1

The memory of the just is blessed,
but the name of the wicked shall rot.
VERSE 7

Hatred stirs up strife, but love covers all sins.
VERSE 12

Verses for Further Memorization/Meditation

- Behold, children are a heritage from the Lord, and the fruit of the womb is His reward (Psalm 127:3).
- And whatever you do, do it heartily, as to the Lord, and not to men, knowing that from the Lord you shall receive the reward of the inheritance, for you serve the Lord Christ (Colossians 3:23–24).
- A good name is better than precious ointment, and the day of death than the day of one's birth (Ecclesiastes 7:1).
- For he who sows to his flesh shall of the flesh reap corruption, but he who sows to the Spirit shall of the Spirit reap life everlasting (Galatians 6:8).
- And above all things have fervent love among yourselves, for love shall cover the multitude of sins (1 Peter 4:8).

Study 11

PROVERBS 11:4–14, 24–31

These verses provide important lessons about righteousness and the outcome of our choices. Proverbs 11 shows a clear difference between the ungodly and the godly, pointing out that wealth and beauty mean little without integrity and character.

Solomon warned that dishonest riches won't help anyone on judgment day, highlighting the inevitable downfall of those driven by greed and deceit. In contrast, the righteous are generous and aligned with God's will, leading to a meaningful life. That should be the desire of every Christian.

We are encouraged to seek righteousness, the true wealth that comes from character and generosity, not from a bank balance or material possessions. This is exactly what the ultimate Son of David—Jesus—would later preach as He walked the earth.

PROVERBS 11:4–14, 24–31 OUTLINE

(VERSE 4)	The ultimate value of righteousness
(VERSES 5–8)	Guidance of the righteous versus the fall of the wicked
(VERSES 9–11)	The power of the mouth's speech
(VERSES 12–14)	The importance of discretion
(VERSES 24–27)	The blessings of generosity
(VERSES 28–29)	Consequences of trusting the wrong things
(VERSES 30–31)	Life-giving wisdom

Contrast of Righteousness and Wickedness, Continued

4Riches do not profit in the day of wrath, but righteousness delivers from death.

5The righteousness of the perfect shall direct his way, but the wicked shall fall by his own wickedness.

6The righteousness of the upright shall deliver them, but transgressors shall be taken in their own wickedness.

7When a wicked man dies, his expectation shall perish, and the hope of unjust men perishes.

8The righteous is delivered out of trouble, and the wicked comes in his place.

9A hypocrite destroys his neighbor with his mouth, but through knowledge the just shall be delivered.

10When it goes well with the righteous, the city rejoices, and when the wicked perish, there is shouting.

11By the blessing of the upright, the city is exalted, but it is overthrown by the mouth of the wicked.

12He who is void of wisdom despises his neighbor, but a man of understanding keeps silent.

13A talebearer reveals secrets, but he who is of a faithful spirit conceals the matter.

14Where there is no counsel, the people fall, but in the multitude of counselors, there is safety. . . .

24There is one who scatters and yet increases, and there is one who withholds more than is right, but it tends to poverty.

25The generous soul shall be made prosperous, and he who waters shall also be watered himself.

26The people shall curse him who withholds grain, but blessing shall be on the head of him who sells it.

27He who diligently seeks good procures favor, but evil shall come to him who seeks it.

28He who trusts in his riches shall fall, but the righteous

shall flourish like a branch.
29He who troubles his own house shall inherit the wind, and the fool shall be servant to the wise of heart.
30The fruit of the righteous is a tree of life, and he who wins souls is wise.
31Behold, the righteous shall be repaid on the earth, much more the wicked and the sinner.

Observe

What do righteousness and wickedness accomplish in people's lives?

....

....

....

....

....

....

How do wise and foolish people speak and treat others?

....

....

....

....

....

....

What does Proverbs 11 have to say about money and different people's attitudes toward it?

Interpret

How is it that the righteous are "delivered" (verse 8) while the wicked fall by their own wickedness?

What does Solomon mean when he says, "He who waters shall also be watered himself" (verse 25)? What aspects of life does this truth apply to?

What does it mean for the righteous to produce "fruit" (verse 30)? How does this relate to winning souls?

Are there any "wicked" ways in your daily life? What can you do to replace them with wise ways?

....

....

....

....

....

....

In what ways might you be unintentionally causing trouble in your own home? What steps can you take to promote harmony instead?

....

....

....

....

....

How can you actively share your faith and contribute to the spiritual growth of others in your community?

....

....

....

....

....

....

PROVERBS 11:4–14, 24–31
SCRIPTURES FOR MEMORIZATION/ MEDITATION

The generous soul shall be made prosperous,
and he who waters shall also be watered himself.
VERSE 25

The fruit of the righteous is a tree of life,
and he who wins souls is wise.
VERSE 30

VERSES FOR FURTHER MEMORIZATION/MEDITATION

- The LORD rewarded me according to my righteousness. He has repaid me according to the cleanness of my hands (2 Samuel 22:21).
- And this also is a great evil, that in all points as he came, so he shall go. And what profit does he who has labored for the wind have? (Ecclesiastes 5:16).
- They shall cast their silver in the streets, and their gold shall be removed; their silver and their gold shall not be able to deliver them in the day of the wrath of the LORD. They shall not satisfy their souls or fill their stomachs, because it is the stumbling block of their iniquity (Ezekiel 7:19).
- Blessed are the merciful, for they shall obtain mercy (Matthew 5:7).
- And the disciples were astonished at His words. But Jesus answered again and said to them, "Children, how hard is it for those who trust in riches to enter into the kingdom of God!" (Mark 10:24).

Study 12

PROVERBS 12:9–28

In a world where wealth seems more important than godliness, a simple life with basic comforts is actually far better than pretending to be rich. Real success comes by working hard, not by putting on airs or looking to get-rich-quick schemes.

Godly people show their true character through kindness and care—and not only for fellow human beings. Caring for working animals is a stewardship responsibility from God and part of righteous living.

Honesty is always the best policy: Reckless words cause problems, but speaking the truth brings peace. Prudent speech and encouraging words are good for all involved and demonstrate "the way of righteousness" (verse 28).

PROVERBS 12:9–28 OUTLINE

(VERSES 9–11)	Stewardship toward oneself, animals, and land
(VERSE 12)	Wickedness ensnares; righteousness yields fruit
(VERSES 13–14)	Words and their consequences
(VERSES 15–16)	Wisdom versus foolishness
(VERSES 17–19)	The power of speech
(VERSES 20–22)	Evil, deceit, contrasted with truthfulness—the Lord's delight
(VERSES 23–28)	Characteristics of a life of wisdom and righteousness

Contrast of Righteousness and Wickedness, Continued

[9]He who is despised and has a servant is better than he who honors himself and lacks bread.

[10]A righteous man regards the life of his beast, but the tender mercies of the wicked are cruel.

[11]He who tills his land shall be satisfied with bread, but he who follows vain people is void of understanding.

[12]The wicked desire the net of evil men, but the root of the righteous yields fruit.

[13]The wicked is snared by the transgression of his lips, but the just shall come out of trouble.

[14]A man shall be satisfied with good by the fruit of his mouth, and the recompense of a man's hands shall be rendered to him.

[15]The way of a fool is right in his own eyes, but he who listens to counsel is wise.

[16]A fool's wrath is presently known, but a prudent man covers shame.

[17]He who speaks truth declares righteousness, but a false witness deceit.

[18]There is one who speaks like the piercings of a sword, but the tongue of the wise is health.

[19]The lips of truth shall be established forever, but a lying tongue is but for a moment.

[20]Deceit is in the heart of those who imagine evil, but to the counselors of peace is joy.

[21]No evil shall happen to the just, but the wicked shall be filled with evil.

[22]Lying lips are an abomination to the LORD, but those who deal truly are His delight.

[23]A prudent man conceals knowledge, but the heart of fools proclaims foolishness.

[24]The hand of the diligent shall rule, but the slothful shall serve as forced laborers.

[25]Heaviness in the heart of man makes it stoop, but a good word makes it glad.

[26]The righteous is more excellent than his neighbor, but the way of the wicked seduces them.

[27]The slothful man does not roast what he took in hunting, but the wealth of a diligent man is precious.

[28]In the way of righteousness is life, and in its pathway there is no death.

Observe

How are righteous, just, and wise people described? What do they do and achieve?

....

....

....

....

....

How does Solomon contrast truth and lies?

....

....

....

....

....

What are the consequences of harmful words? What do wise words accomplish?

Interpret

What do you think Solomon meant in verse 9? How does that relate to today's world?

How can caring for animals—pets, livestock, or wild animals—reflect a person's moral character? Why?

How does hard work lead to leadership, while laziness leads to being a servant?

How honest, encouraging, and wise is your everyday speech? Are there any areas of need you should address?

How well do you "listen to counsel" (verse 15)? How might you do better?

How can the lessons of this chapter help you to reach your life goals?

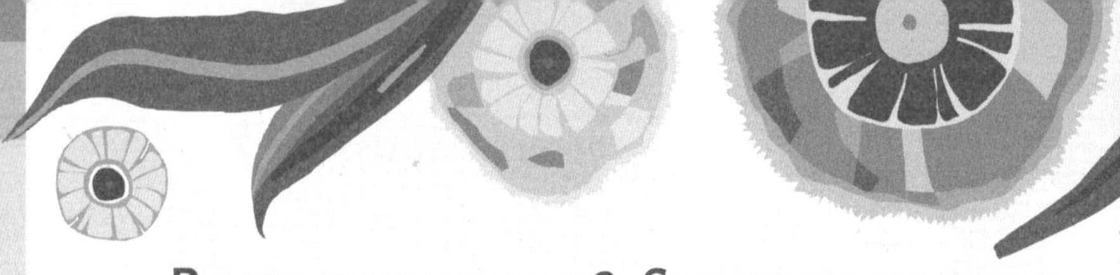

Proverbs 12:9–28 Scriptures for Memorization/Meditation

A righteous man regards the life of his beast,
but the tender mercies of the wicked are cruel.
VERSE 10

There is one who speaks like the piercings of a
sword, but the tongue of the wise is health.
VERSE 18

Verses for Further Memorization/Meditation

- And God said, "Let Us make man in Our image, according to Our likeness, and let them have dominion over the fish of the sea, and over the fowl of the air, and over the cattle, and over all the earth, and over every creeping thing that creeps on the earth" (Genesis 1:26).
- "The Lord God has given Me the tongue of the learned, that I should know how to speak a word in season to him who is weary. He awakens morning by morning. He awakens My ear to hear as the learned" (Isaiah 50:4).
- Let no corrupt communication proceed out of your mouth, but what is good for the use of edifying, that it may minister grace to the hearers (Ephesians 4:29).
- To speak evil of no man, to be not brawlers but gentle, showing all meekness to all men (Titus 3:2).
- Out of the same mouth proceed blessing and cursing. My brothers, these things ought not to be so (James 3:10).

Study 13

PROVERBS 13:4–25

This chapter of Proverbs continues the important themes of the contrast between diligence and laziness. Those who work hard reap rewards, while those who seek gain without effort will ultimately be left wanting. Wealth is deceptive—while riches may provide temporary security, wisdom brings eternal security and fulfillment.

Discipline is portrayed as an act of love, shaping a child's character and future. Good parents leave an inheritance that continues to their grandchildren's generation.

Proverbs 13:4–25 Outline

(VERSE 4)	The sluggard and the diligent
(VERSES 5–6)	Integrity versus dishonesty and wickedness
(VERSES 7–11)	The deceptive nature of worldly wealth
(VERSE 12)	The blessing of fulfilled hope
(VERSES 13–16)	Prudence and knowledge overcome foolishness
(VERSE 17)	The responsibility of faithful representation
(VERSES 18–19)	Honor and fulfillment
(VERSES 20–21)	The impact of friends, whether good or bad
(VERSES 22–24)	Wise stewardship in the family realm
(VERSE 25)	Satisfaction through righteous living

Contrast of Righteousness and Wickedness, Continued

4The soul of the sluggard desires and has nothing, but the soul of the diligent shall be made prosperous.

5A righteous man hates lying, but a wicked man is loathsome and comes to shame.

6Righteousness keeps him who is upright in the way, but wickedness overthrows the sinner.

7There is one who makes himself rich, yet has nothing; there is one who makes himself poor, yet has great riches.

8The ransom of a man's life are his riches, but the poor does not hear rebuke.

9The light of the righteous rejoices, but the lamp of the wicked shall be put out.

10By pride comes only contention, but wisdom is with the well-advised.

11Wealth gotten by dishonesty shall be diminished, but he who gathers by labor shall increase.

12Hope deferred makes the heart sick, but when the desire comes, it is a tree of life.

13Whoever despises the word shall be destroyed, but he who fears the commandment shall be rewarded.

14The law of the wise is a fountain of life, to depart from the snares of death.

15Good understanding gives favor, but the way of transgressors is hard.

16Every prudent man deals with knowledge, but a fool lays open his foolishness.

17A wicked messenger falls into evil, but a faithful ambassador brings health.

18Poverty and shame shall come to him who refuses instruction, but he who regards rebuke shall be honored.

19The desire accomplished is sweet to the soul, but it is

an abomination to fools to depart from evil.
[20]He who walks with wise men shall be wise, but a companion of fools shall be destroyed.
[21]Evil pursues sinners, but good shall be repaid to the
righteous.
[22]A good man leaves an inheritance to his children's children, and the wealth of the sinner is laid up for the just.
[23]Much food is in the cultivated land of the poor, but it is
destroyed for lack of judgment.
[24]He who spares his rod hates his son, but he who loves
him disciplines him promptly.
[25]The righteous eats to the satisfying of his soul, but the
belly of the wicked shall be in need.

Observe

According to this passage, how do wise and hardworking people differ from the lazy and foolish?

....

....

....

....

....

What advice does Solomon provide to parents and families?

....

....

....

....

What are the pros and cons of wealth in this chapter of Proverbs?

....

....

....

Interpret

What all can the term "inheritance" (verse 22) include?

....

....

....

....

How might the phrase "much food" (verse 23) be interpreted in both a literal and figurative sense?

....

....

....

....

Why would Solomon use a messenger as an example of faithfulness or wickedness (verse 17)? How does the messenger idea apply to Christians today?

....

....

....

....

....

Apply

When has laziness—your own or someone else's—affected your life? What did you learn from that experience?

What is your attitude toward building wealth? How are you pursuing that?

How does Solomon's teaching on wise choices apply to modern communication technology? How are you representing Jesus in that realm?

Proverbs 13:4–25 Scripture for Memorization/Meditation

He who spares his rod hates his son, but he who loves him disciplines him promptly.
VERSE 24

Verses for Further Memorization/Meditation

- Many sorrows shall be to the wicked, but he who trusts in the LORD, mercy shall surround him (Psalm 32:10).
- "And now, brothers, I commend you to God and to the word of His grace, which is able to build you up and to give you an inheritance among all those who are sanctified" (Acts 20:32).
- And not only so, but we also glory in tribulations, knowing that tribulation works patience, and patience experience, and experience hope (Romans 5:3–4).
- Do not be deceived: "Evil company corrupts good manners" (1 Corinthians 15:33).
- Do not be deceived; God is not mocked, for whatever a man sows, that he shall also reap (Galatians 6:7).
- And whatever you do, do it heartily, as to the Lord, and not to men, knowing that from the Lord you shall receive the reward of the inheritance, for you serve the Lord Christ (Colossians 3:23–24).
- Now no chastening seems to be joyous for the present, but grievous; nevertheless, afterward it yields the peaceful fruit of righteousness to those who are exercised by it (Hebrews 12:11).

Study 14

PROVERBS 14:1, 12, 17, 20–35

While it speaks of a woman, the opening verse of Proverbs 14 is universally important. Men should also be building up, not tearing down, their own homes.

The contrasts of wisdom and foolishness continue throughout the chapter. Wealth may bring attention and "friends," but true blessings come from being kind to all, regardless of their financial situation. Hard work, as we have already seen, leads to success, while laziness leads to nothing good.

Of particular import is that a nation's success depends on the value of its people as much as its leaders. God's wisdom shapes both personal lives and the future of a nation.

PROVERBS 14:1, 12, 17, 20–35 OUTLINE

(VERSE 1)	Womanly wisdom: the key to a strong home
(VERSE 12)	Human wisdom is unreliable; God's is everything
(VERSE 17)	Controlling emotions is crucial to wise living
(VERSES 20–22)	The value of kindness to all
(VERSES 23–24)	Effort and reward
(VERSE 25)	The impact of honest testimony
(VERSE 26)	A safe haven in God
(VERSE 27)	Life-giving benefits of revering the Lord
(VERSES 28–35)	The moral fabric of a nation: citizens and rulers

The Contrast of Goodness and Evil

1 Every wise woman builds her house, but the foolish plucks it
down with her hands. . . .
12 There is a way that seems right to a man, but the end of
it are the ways of death. . . .
17 He who is quickly angered deals foolishly, and a man of
wicked devices is hated. . . .
20 The poor is hated even by his own neighbor, but the rich
has many friends.
21 He who despises his neighbor sins, but he who has mercy
on the poor is happy.
22 Do they not go astray who devise evil? But mercy and
truth shall be to those who devise good.
23 In all labor there is profit, but the talk of the lips tends
only to poverty.
24 The crown of the wise is their riches, but the foolishness
of fools is foolishness.
25 A true witness delivers souls, but a deceitful witness
speaks lies.
26 In the fear of the Lord is strong confidence, and His
children shall have a place of refuge.
27 The fear of the Lord is a fountain of life, to depart from
the snares of death.
28 In the multitude of people is the king's honor, but in the
lack of people is the destruction of the prince.
29 He who is slow to wrath has great understanding, but
he who is quick-tempered exalts foolishness.
30 A sound heart is the life of the flesh, but envy the rottenness
of the bones.
31 He who oppresses the poor discredits his Maker, but he
who honors Him has mercy on the poor.
32 The wicked is driven away in his wickedness, but the

righteous has hope in his death.
[33]Wisdom rests in the heart of him who has understanding,
but what is in the midst of fools is made known.
[34]Righteousness exalts a nation, but sin is a reproach to
any people.
[35]The king's favor is toward a wise servant, but his wrath
is against him who causes shame.

Observe

What do verses 1, 12, and 17 have in common? How do they differ?

Beside the general categories of wise and foolish, what specific kinds of people are mentioned in this passage? What do we learn about them?

What does Solomon say about national leaders and their people in verses 28–35? How do wisdom and righteousness benefit each?

....

....

....

Interpret

How and why would foolish people "pluck down" their house? What does it take to "build" a house?

....

....

....

....

What is the way that "seems right" (verse 12) but actually leads to death?

....

....

....

....

How and why would righteousness exalt a nation (verse 34)? How is sin a reproach, or disgrace?

....

....

....

....

Apply

What specific actions can you take to build up your home, church, or community? What specific things should you be avoiding?

In what ways can you build real friendships that are not based on money, popularity, or other worldly attractions?

How can you contribute to the righteousness of your nation?

Proverbs 14:1, 12, 17, 20–35 Scriptures for Memorization/ Meditation

There is a way that seems right to a man,
but the end of it are the ways of death.
VERSE 12

In the multitude of people is the king's honor, but in the lack of people is the destruction of the prince.
VERSE 28

Verses for Further Memorization/Meditation

- "If My people who are called by My name shall humble themselves and pray and seek My face and turn from their wicked ways, then I will hear from heaven and will forgive their sin and will heal their land" (2 Chronicles 7:14).
- And wisdom and knowledge shall be the stability of your times, and strength of salvation. The fear of the LORD is his treasure (Isaiah 33:6).
- Therefore, my beloved brothers, let every man be swift to hear, slow to speak, slow to anger. For the anger of man does not work the righteousness of God (James 1:19–20).
- "His lord said to him, 'Well done, good and faithful servant. You have been faithful over a few things; I will make you ruler over many things. Enter into the joy of your lord'" (Matthew 25:21).

Study 15

PROVERBS 15:1–20

Gentle, truthful, appealing speech is a virtue of wisdom and builds good relationships. God knows what we think and say, and He rewards those who treasure righteousness.

Solomon reminds us that God allows foolish people to face the consequences of their choices. Those who refuse to repent, rejecting His correction, will "die"—spiritually and perhaps even physically. So everyone should focus on their own heart attitudes. No one can control what happens to them, but we should all endeavor to respond wisely and well in accordance with God's truth.

Wisdom is derived from understanding life from God's perspective. This leads to happiness, which is a feast of joy, love, and the fear of the Lord.

Proverbs 15:1–20 Outline

(VERSES 1–4)	The virtue of wise, peaceful communication
(VERSES 5–7)	Wisdom and instruction build homes
(VERSES 8–9)	God values righteousness over empty rituals
(VERSES 10–12)	Rejecting wisdom leads to ultimate destruction
(VERSES 13–14)	True wisdom comes from within
(VERSES 15–17)	A happy heart enjoys endless blessings
(VERSES 18–19)	Righteousness and diligence lead to fulfillment
(VERSE 20)	Wisdom and respect in family dynamics

The Contrast of Goodness and Evil, Continued

1 A soft answer turns away wrath, but harsh words stir up anger.

2 The tongue of the wise uses knowledge rightly, but the mouth of fools pours out foolishness.

3 The eyes of the LORD are in every place, watching the evil and the good.

4 A wholesome tongue is a tree of life, but perverseness in it is a breach in the spirit.

5 A fool despises his father's instruction, but he who regards correction is prudent.

6 In the house of the righteous is much treasure, but in the revenues of the wicked is trouble.

7 The lips of the wise disperse knowledge, but the heart of the foolish does not do so.

8 The sacrifice of the wicked is an abomination to the LORD, but the prayer of the upright is His delight.

9 The way of the wicked is an abomination to the LORD, but He loves him who follows after righteousness.

10 Correction is harsh to him who forsakes the way, and he who hates rebuke shall die.

11 Hell and destruction are before the LORD. How much more, then, the hearts of the children of men?

12 A scorner does not love one who rebukes him, nor will he go to the wise.

13 A merry heart makes a cheerful face, but by sorrow of the heart the spirit is broken.

14 The heart of him who has understanding seeks knowledge, but the mouth of fools feeds on foolishness.

15 All the days of the afflicted are evil, but he who is of a merry heart has a continual feast.

16 Better is little with the fear of the LORD than great treasure and trouble with it.

[17]Better is a dinner of vegetables where love is than a fattened ox and hatred with it.

[18]A wrathful man stirs up strife, but he who is slow to anger appeases strife.

[19]The way of the slothful man is like a hedge of thorns, but the way of the righteous is made plain.

[20]A wise son makes a glad father, but a foolish man despises his mother.

Observe

What kinds of speech are mentioned in Proverbs 15? What is the impact of each type?

....

....

....

....

....

According to this chapter, what kinds of things do wicked people do? What are the consequences?

....

....

....

....

....

....

What positive attitudes and behaviors are mentioned in Proverbs 15? How do they benefit a person?

Interpret

Why are correction and rebuke so important in this passage?

What does it mean for someone to have a "merry heart" (verse 13)? What about a broken spirit?

Why is the fear of the Lord better than tangible wealth (verse 16)? Is it possible to have both?

Apply

How have you responded when faced with godly correction? How did that play out?

What can you do to respect your parents' guidance, however old you may be now?

How good are you at providing "a soft answer" (verse 1) to angry words? How might you improve in this area?

Proverbs 15:1–20 Scriptures for Memorization/Meditation

A soft answer turns away wrath,
but harsh words stir up anger.
VERSE 1

The eyes of the LORD are in every place,
watching the evil and the good.
VERSE 3

Verses for Further Memorization/Meditation

- Guard your steps when you go to the house of God, and be more ready to hear than to give the sacrifice of fools. For they do not consider that they do evil (Ecclesiastes 5:1).
- A little that a righteous man has is better than the riches of many wicked (Psalm 37:16).
- If I ascend up into heaven, You are there. If I make my bed in hell, behold, You are there (Psalm 139:8).
- Blessed are the pure in heart, for they shall see God (Matthew 5:8).
- Not that I speak in respect of need, for I have learned in whatever state I am to be content with it (Philippians 4:11).
- But godliness with contentment is great gain (1 Timothy 6:6).
- Therefore, my beloved brothers, let every man be swift to hear, slow to speak, slow to anger (James 1:19).

Study 16

PROVERBS 16:3, 8–9, 14–32

Life is full of choices, and here Solomon offers wisdom on making the right ones.

Trusting God with your plans leads to success. But success isn't just money and things—in fact, it's far more than just that. Success, in God's sight, is being righteous. Choosing positive though intangible qualities over worldly wealth requires humility and trust in the Lord.

Proverbs 16:3, 8–9, 14–32 Outline

(VERSE 3)	Trust God with your entire life
(VERSE 8)	Righteousness excels unjust riches
(VERSE 9)	God directs human lives
(VERSES 14–15)	Act wisely around leaders, who are simply human beings as well
(VERSES 16–17)	It's better to choose wisdom over tangible wealth
(VERSES 18–19)	Humility is better than pride
(VERSES 20–24)	Wise words bring joy in life
(VERSE 25)	Godly wisdom in decision-making
(VERSES 26–30)	The consequences of foolishness and deception
(VERSE 31)	The glory of righteous aging
(VERSE 32)	Self-control is a wise and valuable power

The Contrast of Goodness and Evil, Continued

3 Commit your works to the Lord and your thoughts shall be established. . . .

8 Better is a little with righteousness than great revenues without justice.

9 A man's heart devises his way, but the Lord directs his steps. . . .

14 The wrath of a king is like messengers of death, but a wise man will pacify it.

15 In the light of the king's face is life, and his favor is like a cloud of the latter rain.

16 How much better is it to get wisdom than gold! And to get understanding is to be chosen rather than silver!

17 The highway of the upright is to depart from evil; he who keeps his way preserves his soul.

18 Pride goes before destruction, and a haughty spirit before a fall.

19 It is better to be of a humble spirit with the lowly than to divide the plunder with the proud.

20 He who handles a matter wisely shall find good, and whoever trusts in the Lord, happy is he.

21 The wise in heart shall be called prudent, and the sweetness of the lips increases learning.

22 Understanding is a wellspring of life to him who has it, but the instruction of fools is foolishness.

23 The heart of the wise teaches his mouth and adds learning to his lips.

24 Pleasant words are like a honeycomb, sweet to the soul and health to the bones.

25 There is a way that seems right to a man, but the end of it are the ways of death.

26 He who labors, labors for himself, for his mouth craves it of him.

[27]An ungodly man digs up evil, and in his lips there is a
burning fire.
[28]A perverse man sows strife, and a whisperer separates
close friends.
[29]A violent man entices his neighbor and leads him into
the way that is not good.
[30]He shuts his eyes to devise perverse things; moving his
lips, he brings evil to pass.
[31]The gray head is a crown of glory, if it is found in the
way of righteousness.
[32]He who is slow to anger is better than the mighty, and
he who rules his spirit than he who takes a city.

Observe

What is God's role in human planning and progress?

....

....

....

....

....

What happens to people who are careless, prideful, and wicked?

....

....

....

....

How are wise people described in these verses? What becomes of them?

Interpret

What does it mean to "commit your works to the LORD" (verse 3)? How can you do that?

What lessons can we learn from the phrase "there is a way that seems right to a man" (verse 25)?

Why might the idea of "the gray head" (verse 31) be placed where it is? What do you think Solomon was implying?

Apply

How much does this world value righteousness over material things? How much do you?

How can you keep pride and "a haughty spirit" (verse 18) at bay in your own life?

How can you use your words to truthfully encourage and uplift those around you?

Proverbs 16:3, 8–9, 14–32 Scriptures for Memorization/ Meditation

A man's heart devises his way,
but the Lord directs his steps.
VERSE 9

The gray head is a crown of glory, if it is
found in the way of righteousness.
VERSE 31

Verses for Further Memorization/Meditation

- A little that a righteous man has is better than the riches of many wicked (Psalm 37:16).
- And a highway shall be there, and a way, and it shall be called the Way of Holiness. The unclean shall not pass over it, but it shall be for others. The traveling men, though fools, shall not go astray on it (Isaiah 35:8).
- O Lord, I know that the way of man is not in himself; it is not in man who walks to direct his steps (Jeremiah 10:23).
- "For what shall it profit a man if he gains the whole world and loses his own soul?" (Mark 8:36).
- Let no corrupt communication proceed out of your mouth, but what is good for the use of edifying, that it may minister grace to the hearers (Ephesians 4:29).

Study 17

PROVERBS 17:1–22

Solomon, a man of incredible riches, understood that a simple life filled with peace is far better than great wealth that brings conflict. True happiness comes from God's blessing, not from owning all the things of this world.

Solomon recognized that relationships can be saved or destroyed depending on what is said or not said—that true friends are those who love and support you through all circumstances. Wise people learn from correction, while fools refuse to change.

PROVERBS 17:1–22 OUTLINE

(VERSE 1)	Peace is better than material abundance
(VERSE 2)	A wise servant outshines a foolish son
(VERSE 3)	God tries human hearts like gold in a furnace
(VERSES 4–10)	The importance of respectful words in human relationships
(VERSES 11–12)	There is danger in rebellion and folly
(VERSES 13–14)	The results of evil and strife
(VERSES 15–16)	Injustice and foolishness
(VERSES 17–18)	The blessings and dangers of friendship
(VERSES 19–20)	The consequences of dishonesty and selfishness
(VERSES 21–22)	Children can bring sorrow or joy

The Contrast of Goodness and Evil, Continued

[1]Better is a dry morsel with quietness than a house full of sacrifices with strife.

[2]A wise servant shall have rule over a son who causes shame and shall have part of the inheritance among the brothers.

[3]The refining pot is for silver and the furnace for gold, but the LORD tries the hearts.

[4]A wicked doer gives heed to false lips, and a liar gives ear to an evil tongue.

[5]Whoever mocks the poor discredits his Maker, and he who is glad at calamities shall not be unpunished.

[6]Children's children are the crown of old men, and the glory of children are their fathers.

[7]Excellent speech does not become a fool, much less do lying lips a prince.

[8]A gift is like a precious stone in the eyes of him who has it; wherever it turns, it prospers.

[9]He who covers a transgression seeks love, but he who repeats a matter separates close friends.

[10]A rebuke enters more into a wise man than a hundred lashes into a fool.

[11]An evil man seeks only rebellion; therefore, a cruel messenger shall be sent against him.

[12]Let a bear robbed of her cubs meet a man, rather than a fool in his foolishness.

[13]Whoever rewards evil for good, evil shall not depart from his house.

[14]The beginning of strife is like when one lets out water; therefore, leave off contention, before it is meddled with.

[15]He who justifies the wicked and he who condemns the just, they are both an abomination to the LORD.

[16]Why is there a price in the hand of a fool to get wisdom,

since he has no heart for it?
17A friend loves at all times, and a brother is born for
adversity.
18A man void of understanding shakes hands and becomes
surety in the presence of his friend.
19He who loves strife loves transgression, and he who
exalts his gate seeks destruction.
20He who has a perverse heart finds no good, and he who
has a perverse tongue falls into evil.
21He who fathers a fool does it to his sorrow, and the father
of a fool has no joy.
22A merry heart does good like a medicine, but a broken
spirit dries the bones.

Observe

According to Solomon, the wealthiest man who ever lived, what things are better than wealth?

....

....

....

....

....

What does this chapter say brings joy and satisfaction to life? What brings the opposite?

....

....

....

What are the qualities of true friends?

Interpret

What does the phrase “a brother is born for adversity” (verse 17) suggest? Who is “a brother”?

What did Solomon mean by saying it is better to face “a bear robbed of her cubs” (verse 12) than a person lacking wisdom and good judgment?

Why would mocking the poor “discredit” God (verse 5)?

What is God saying specifically to your response to disagreements and strife in your life?

How can you guard against having a "perverse" heart and tongue (verse 20)?

How can you be a friend who "loves at all times" (verse 17)? What might need to change in your life to achieve that level of love?

Proverbs 17:1–22 Scriptures for Memorization/Meditation

Better is a dry morsel with quietness than
a house full of sacrifices with strife.
VERSE 1

A friend loves at all times, and a
brother is born for adversity.
VERSE 17

A merry heart does good like a medicine,
but a broken spirit dries the bones.
VERSE 22

Verses for Further Memorization/Meditation

- And Ruth said, "Do not entreat me to leave you or to return from following after you, for where you go, I will go, and where you lodge, I will lodge. Your people shall be my people, and your God my God" (Ruth 1:16).
- But no man can tame the tongue; it is an unruly evil, full of deadly poison (James 3:8).
- But whoever has this world's goods and sees his brother in need and shuts up his heart of compassion from him, how does the love of God dwell in him? (1 John 3:17).
- If a man says "I love God" and hates his brother, he is a liar, for how can he who does not love his brother, whom he has seen, love God, whom he has not seen? And we have this commandment from Him: that he who loves God also love his brother (1 John 4:20–21).

Study 18

PROVERBS 18:10–24

Throughout the Proverbs, much emphasis is put on spoken words—and for a good reason. What we say has tremendous power—our words can nourish and uplift like satisfying food, or they can cast people down to the very depths of despair.

Of course, words affect our relationships, another important theme in Solomon's writings. Our choice of friends displays either wisdom or folly, as does our pursuit of a spouse. While the Proverbs identify a wife as a "good thing" and a source of "favor from the Lord" (verse 22), this is also certainly true of a woman who obtains a good husband. With regard to our friendships, Solomon hints that those with many friends can be led astray by some of their many acquaintances. But true, godly, wise friends can actually become much closer to us than our family relationships.

Proverbs 18:10–24 Outline

(verses 10–11)	True security comes from God, not wealth
(verses 12–13)	Patience and humility are the path to honor
(verse 14)	A healthy spirit heals
(verses 15, 17)	The wise seek knowledge
(verse 16)	Use your God-given talents for good
(verse 18)	Fairness helps to resolve disputes
(verses 19, 22)	Family harmony is vital
(verses 20–21)	Words can heal or destroy
(verses 23–24)	Human kindness and true friendship

The Contrast of Goodness and Evil, Continued

10 The name of the Lord is a strong tower. The righteous runs
into it and is safe.

11 The rich man's wealth is his strong city, and like a high
wall in his own opinion.

12 Before destruction the heart of man is haughty, and
before honor is humility.

13 He who answers a matter before he hears it, it is folly
and shame to him.

14 The spirit of a man will sustain his sickness, but who can
bear a wounded spirit?

15 The heart of the prudent gets knowledge, and the ear of
the wise seeks knowledge.

16 A man's gift makes room for him and brings him before
great men.

17 He who is first in his own cause seems just, but his
neighbor comes and searches him.

18 The lot causes contentions to cease and apportions
between the mighty.

19 A brother offended is harder to be won than a strong
city, and their contentions are like the bars of a castle.

20 A man's belly shall be satisfied with the fruit of his mouth,
and with the increase of his lips he shall be filled.

21 Death and life are in the power of the tongue, and those
who love it shall eat its fruit.

22 Whoever finds a wife finds a good thing and obtains
favor from the Lord.

23 The poor uses entreaties, but the rich answers roughly.

24 A man who has friends must show himself friendly, and
there is a friend who sticks closer than a brother.

Observe

What effects, both positive and negative, do our words produce?

What guidance does Solomon provide for our human relationships?

According to this passage, how does haughtiness appear? What are its consequences?

Interpret

Why would "a brother offended" be harder to win than "a strong city" (verse 19)?

How might verse 17 relate to testimony in a court trial? How would you rephrase this verse in your own words?

Is every spouse "a good thing" (verse 22)? Why or why not?

How do you run to the Lord for safety as your "strong tower" (verse 10)?

What does "the fruit of [your] mouth" taste like (verse 20)? How satisfying is it to you and to others?

How would you compare your relationships with family members to those with friends? Could you "show yourself friendlier" (verse 21) to any relatives?

Proverbs 18:10–24 Scriptures for Memorization/Meditation

Death and life are in the power of the tongue,
and those who love it shall eat its fruit.
VERSE 21

A man who has friends must show himself friendly,
and there is a friend who sticks closer than a brother.
VERSE 24

Verses for Further Memorization/Meditation

- Therefore a man shall leave his father and his mother and shall cleave to his wife, and they shall be one flesh (Genesis 2:24).
- God is our refuge and strength, a very present help in trouble (Psalm 46:1).
- "For by your words you shall be justified, and by your words you shall be condemned" (Matthew 12:37).
- "And the King shall answer and say to them, 'Truly I say to you, because you have done it to one of the least of these My brothers, you have done it to Me'" (Matthew 25:40).
- "Therefore if you bring your gift to the altar, and there remember that your brother has anything against you, leave your gift there before the altar, and go your way. First be reconciled to your brother, and then come and offer your gift" (Matthew 5:23–24).
- So men ought to love their wives as their own bodies. He who loves his wife loves himself (Ephesians 5:28).

Study 19

PROVERBS 20:1–3, 15–30

Proverbs 20 offers important lessons on wisdom in daily life. Avoid drunkenness; it is a very dangerous thing. Don't provoke those in power; this is a sin against yourself. Steer clear of strife; only fools meddle in conflict.

Solomon also counsels against assuming debts carelessly, gossiping, cursing one's parents, and cheating in business. It is essential to live openly and honestly before God, as He knows our hearts and oversees our ways.

Aging is presented as a positive thing. We can celebrate the wisdom that comes with being granted many years, recognizing that our life experiences—even the painful ones—have helped us to grow stronger and to resist evil.

PROVERBS 20:1–3, 15–30 OUTLINE

(VERSES 1–3)	Wisdom is to avoid unnecessary conflict
(VERSE 15)	The precious value of wisdom
(VERSE 16)	A caution against taking on debts
(VERSES 17–19)	Poor choices have consequences
(VERSES 20–21)	Dishonor in families is serious
(VERSES 22–27)	Justice, integrity, and divine oversight in human affairs
(VERSE 28)	Kindness and integrity in leadership
(VERSE 29)	Embracing each age in life
(VERSE 30)	Painful experiences bring growth

Warnings and Instructions

1 Wine is a mocker; strong drink is raging, and whoever is deceived by it is not wise.

2 The wrath of a king is like the roaring of a lion; whoever provokes him to anger sins against his own soul.

3 It is an honor for a man to cease from strife, but every fool will be meddling. . . .

15 There is gold and a multitude of rubies, but the lips of knowledge are a precious jewel.

16 Take the garment of one who is surety for a stranger, and take a pledge from him for a foreign woman.

17 Bread of deceit is sweet to a man, but afterward his mouth shall be filled with gravel.

18 Every purpose is established by counsel, and with good advice make war.

19 He who goes about as a talebearer reveals secrets; therefore, do not meddle with him who flatters with his lips.

20 Whoever curses his father or his mother, his lamp shall be put out in obscure darkness.

21 An inheritance may be gotten hastily at the beginning, but its end shall not be blessed.

22 Do not say, "I will repay evil," but wait on the Lord, and He shall save you.

23 Diverse weights are an abomination to the Lord, and a false balance is not good.

24 Man's steps are of the Lord. How can a man then understand his own way?

25 It is a snare to the man who devours what is holy, and to make inquiry after vows.

26 A wise king scatters the wicked and brings the wheel over them.

27 The spirit of man is the candle of the Lord, searching all the inner parts of the belly.

28Mercy and truth preserve the king, and his throne is
upheld by mercy.
29The glory of young men is their strength, and the beauty
of old men is the gray head.
30The bruising of a wound cleanses away evil, as do lashes
the inner parts of the belly.

Observe

What various images do these verses use to communicate the importance of wisdom?

....

....

....

....

What poor behaviors does Solomon describe in this passage? What are their consequences?

....

....

....

What are Solomon's teachings on money in Proverbs 20?

....

....

....

....

Interpret

What does Solomon mean about people being "deceived" by wine and strong drink (verse 1)?

How and why would someone provoke the wrath of a king (verse 2)? How might this apply to modern democracies?

How do "strength" and "the gray head" compare and contrast in verse 29?

When have you been tempted to involve yourself in strife? How did that turn out?

....

....

....

....

....

....

How open are you to pursuing wise counsel? Who in your life is a good source of that?

....

....

....

....

....

....

What does it mean that "man's [or woman's] steps are of the LORD" (verse 24)? How are your own steps "of the LORD"?

....

....

....

....

....

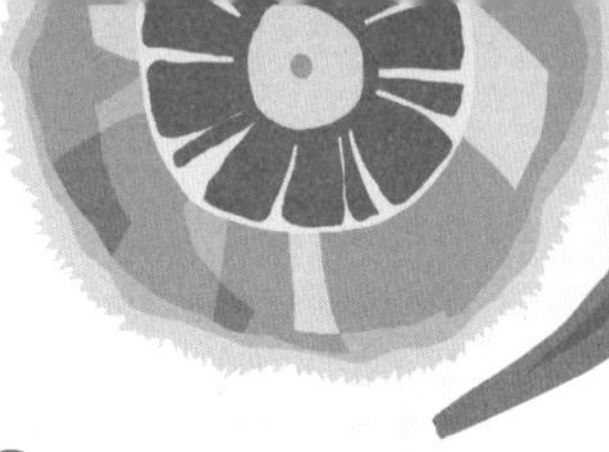

Proverbs 20:1–3, 15–30 Scriptures for Memorization/Meditation

Wine is a mocker; strong drink is raging,
and whoever is deceived by it is not wise.
VERSE 1

The glory of young men is their strength,
and the beauty of old men is the gray head.
VERSE 29

Verses for Further Memorization/Meditation

- I will early destroy all the wicked of the land, that I may cut off all wicked doers from the city of the Lord (Psalm 101:8).
- How often they provoked Him in the wilderness and grieved Him in the desert! (Psalm 78:40).
- Do you not know that the unrighteous shall not inherit the kingdom of God? Do not be deceived; neither fornicators, nor idolaters, nor adulterers, nor effeminate, nor abusers of themselves with mankind, nor thieves, nor covetous, nor drunkards, nor revilers, nor extortioners shall inherit the kingdom of God (1 Corinthians 6:9–10).
- But the wisdom that is from above is first pure, then peaceable, gentle, and easy to reason with; full of mercy and good fruits, without partiality, and without hypocrisy (James 3:17).

Study 20

PROVERBS 21:2–20, 31

It's not enough to simply follow religious rules; true righteousness comes from caring for people the way God does. And we must do this "justice and judgment" (verse 3) even when it seems as if wicked people prosper. In reality, the way of the sinful ultimately leads to trouble. Living with integrity and kindness results in a happy and rewarding life.

Solomon hints at the balance between human effort and divine protection in facing life's challenges. While we must work diligently, it is ultimately God who provides our guidance and safety.

Proverbs 21:2–20, 31 Outline

(VERSES 2–3)	God's sovereignty and justice
(VERSES 4–8)	The consequences of pride and wickedness
(VERSES 9, 19)	Domestic harmony is better than strife
(VERSES 10–12)	The heart and actions of the wicked
(VERSE 13)	There are consequences to ignoring the poor
(VERSE 14)	Short-term solutions to conflict
(VERSES 15–18)	Iniquity, foolishness, and pleasure's consequences
(VERSE 20)	Habits of the foolish and the wise
(VERSE 31)	The balance between human effort and divine protection

Warnings and Instructions, Continued

2 Every way of a man is right in his own eyes, but the Lord ponders the hearts.

3 To do justice and judgment is more acceptable to the Lord than sacrifice.

4 A haughty look and a proud heart and the plowing of the wicked are sin.

5 The thoughts of the diligent tend only to plenty, but of everyone who is hasty, only to want.

6 The getting of treasures by a lying tongue is an idol tossed to and fro by those who seek death.

7 The robbery of the wicked shall destroy them because they refuse to do judgment.

8 The way of man is perverse and strange, but as for the pure, his work is right.

9 It is better to dwell in a corner of the housetop than with a brawling woman in a wide house.

10 The soul of the wicked desires evil; his neighbor finds no favor in his eyes.

11 When the scorner is punished, the simple is made wise, and when the wise is instructed, he receives knowledge.

12 The righteous man wisely considers the house of the wicked, but God overthrows the wicked for their wickedness.

13 Whoever stops his ears at the cry of the poor, he also shall cry himself, but shall not be heard.

14 A gift in secret pacifies anger, and a bribe in the bosom strong wrath.

15 It is joy to the just to do justice, but destruction shall come to the workers of iniquity.

16 The man who wanders out of the way of understanding shall remain in the congregation of the dead.

17 He who loves pleasure shall be a poor man; he who loves

wine and oil shall not be rich.
18The wicked shall be a ransom for the righteous, and the transgressor for the upright.
19It is better to dwell in the wilderness than with a contentious and an angry woman.
20There is treasure to be desired and oil in the dwelling of the wise, but a foolish man swallows it up. . . .
31The horse is prepared for the day of battle, but safety is of the LORD.

Observe

How are "the wicked" described in this passage? What things do the wicked do?

....

....

....

....

....

What words are used in this passage to describe those who are not wicked? What do these people do?

....

....

....

....

....

What does Solomon teach about work and wealth in these verses?

....

....

....

....

Interpret

What does Solomon mean when he states, "the Lord ponders the hearts" (verse 2)?

....

....

....

....

Would you consider verse 13 a threat? Why or why not?

....

....

....

....

Are all who love pleasure and wine poor (verse 17)? What exactly is this verse saying?

....

....

....

....

How can you be sure that your ways are right in God's eyes, not just your own (verse 2)?

What are the "thoughts of the diligent" that "tend only to plenty" (verse 5)? Would they describe your thoughts?

How might the idea that "safety is of the LORD" (verse 31) influence your perspective on the dangers of daily life?

Proverbs 21:2–20, 31 Scriptures for Memorization/Meditation

Every way of a man is right in his own eyes,
but the LORD ponders the hearts.
VERSE 2

The horse is prepared for the day of
battle, but safety is of the LORD.
VERSE 31

Verses for Further Memorization/Meditation

- Some trust in chariots and some in horses, but we will remember the name of the LORD our God (Psalm 20:7).
- Wait on the LORD. Be of good courage, and He shall strengthen your heart. Wait, I say, on the LORD (Psalm 27:14).
- Wealth and riches shall be in his house, and his righteousness endures forever (Psalm 112:3).
- "Not everyone who says to Me, 'Lord, Lord,' shall enter into the kingdom of heaven, but he who does the will of My Father who is in heaven" (Matthew 7:21).
- And He said to them, "You are those who justify yourselves before men, but God knows your hearts. For what is highly esteemed among men is an abomination in the sight of God" (Luke 16:15).
- Do not repay evil for evil to any man. Provide honest things in the sight of all men (Romans 12:17).

Study 21

PROVERBS 22:1–16

Solomon, known for his unparalleled wisdom, highlights the realities of life—how wealth influences power, how generosity brings blessings, and how truth ultimately prevails. Discipline, administered by loving parents, is key to guiding children toward a healthy and productive life. The "rod" refers to a shepherd's tool used for guiding sheep away from dangers—it was not used harshly or in anger.

While Solomon lived under the Old Testament law, we live in the age of grace, where all who believe in Jesus Christ—not just prophets or kings or priests—enjoy His daily presence and wisdom. But Solomon's words remain relevant, providing guidance that the Holy Spirit can use to conduct us toward greater godliness.

Proverbs 22:1–16 Outline

(VERSE 1)	A good name is priceless
(VERSE 2)	Wealth does not define a person's worth
(VERSE 3)	Wisdom is found in caution and foresight
(VERSE 4)	The fear of God is the source of a good life
(VERSE 5)	Perilous paths can and should be avoided
(VERSES 6, 15)	Guiding children toward a good life
(VERSES 7–9)	Wealth, generosity, and consequences
(VERSES 10–12)	Eliminating strife and embracing graciousness
(VERSES 13–14)	The dangers of laziness and temptation
(VERSE 16)	Dangerous financial behaviors

Warnings and Instructions, Continued

[1]A good name is rather to be chosen than great riches, and loving favor rather than silver and gold.

[2]The rich and poor meet together; the Lord is the Maker of them all.

[3]A prudent man foresees the evil and hides himself, but the simple pass on and are punished.

[4]By humility and the fear of the Lord are riches and honor and life.

[5]Thorns and snares are in the way of the perverse; he who guards his soul shall be far from them.

[6]Train up a child in the way he should go, and when he is old, he will not depart from it.

[7]The rich rules over the poor, and the borrower is servant to the lender.

[8]He who sows iniquity shall reap vanity, and the rod of his anger shall fail.

[9]He who has a bountiful eye shall be blessed, for he gives of his bread to the poor.

[10]Cast out the scorner, and contention shall go out; yes, strife and reproach shall cease.

[11]He who loves pureness of heart, for the grace of his lips, the king shall be his friend.

[12]The eyes of the Lord preserve knowledge, and He overthrows the words of the transgressor.

[13]The slothful man says, "There is a lion outside; I shall be slain in the streets."

[14]The mouth of adulterous women is a deep pit; he who is abhorred by the Lord shall fall there.

[15]Foolishness is bound in the heart of a child, but the rod of correction shall drive it far from him.

16He who oppresses the poor to increase his riches and he who gives to the rich shall surely come to want.

Observe

What instructions does Solomon give for child rearing? What will be their results?

What examples of sowing and reaping appear in this passage?

What financial teachings does Solomon provide in Proverbs 22?

Interpret

Why would King Solomon warn his children about the way they treat the wealthy and the poor?

Why and how would "humility and the fear of the Lord" lead to "riches and honor and life" (verse 4)?

According to verses 6 and 15, how do you think children should be disciplined?

Apply

How strongly do you agree with Solomon's statement that "a good name is rather to be chosen than great riches" (verse 1)? Why?

....

....

....

....

....

What steps can you take to show humble respect toward others, regardless of their social or economic status?

....

....

....

....

....

....

When have you experienced Solomon's teaching that "the borrower is servant to the lender" (verse 7)? How can you avoid this kind of servanthood?

....

....

....

....

....

Proverbs 22:1–16 Scriptures for Memorization/Meditation

The rich and poor meet together;
the Lord is the Maker of them all.
VERSE 2

Train up a child in the way he should go,
and when he is old, he will not depart from it.
VERSE 6

Foolishness is bound in the heart of a child,
but the rod of correction shall drive it far from him.
VERSE 15

Verses for Further Memorization/Meditation

- "And these words that I command you this day shall be in your heart. And you shall teach them diligently to your children and shall talk of them when you sit in your house and when you walk by the way and when you lie down and when you rise up" (Deuteronomy 6:6–7).
- A good name is better than precious ointment, and the day of death than the day of one's birth (Ecclesiastes 7:1).
- But I say this: he who sows sparingly shall also reap sparingly, and he who sows bountifully shall also reap bountifully (2 Corinthians 9:6).
- Children, obey your parents in all things, for this is well pleasing to the Lord. Fathers, do not provoke your children to anger, lest they be discouraged (Colossians 3:20–21).

Study 22

PROVERBS 22:17–29

This passage introduces a new section in Proverbs, continuing into chapter 24, that some have called the "Sayings of the Wise." These words come from God-fearing sages and tend to be longer and more structured than Solomon's earlier proverbs. But we will see more from Solomon again later.

That this switch in authors occurs mid-chapter may seem strange to us today. But Proverbs was originally one continuous text—the chapter and verse divisions came much later in time. This section may have been grouped with the beginning of Proverbs 22 because of its similar themes.

These wise sayings warn against taking advantage of the poor, associating with hot-tempered people, and being careless with loans. Subtle types of theft—at that time, moving boundary markers—are discouraged. As is often the case in the Proverbs, we are gently reminded of the worth of working hard, which can lead to great success.

PROVERBS 22:17–29 OUTLINE

(VERSES 17–21)	Introduction to a new section of Proverbs
(VERSES 22–23)	Do not take advantage of the poor
(VERSES 24–25)	Stay away from angry people
(VERSES 26–27)	Avoid risky loans
(VERSE 28)	Do not steal land
(VERSE 29)	Work hard to find success

WARNINGS AND INSTRUCTIONS, CONTINUED

17 Bow down your ear and hear the words of the wise, and apply your heart to my knowledge.

18 For it is a pleasant thing if you keep them within you; they shall be fitted on your lips besides.

19 That your trust may be in the LORD, I have made known to you this day, even to you.

20 Have I not written to you excellent things in counsels and knowledge,

21 that I might make you know the certainty of the words of truth, that you might answer the words of truth to those who send you?

22 Do not rob the poor because he is poor or oppress the afflicted in the gate,

23 for the LORD will plead their case and plunder the soul of those who plundered them.

24 Make no friendship with an angry man, and with a furious man you shall not go,

25 lest you learn his ways and get a snare for your soul.

26 Do not be one of those who shakes hands, or of those who are sureties for debts.

27 If you have nothing to pay, why should he take away your bed from under you?

28 Do not remove the ancient landmark, which your fathers have set.

29 Do you see a man diligent in his business? He shall stand before kings; he shall not stand before obscure men.

Observe

What are we told to do with the words of the wise? What do these words do for us?

What does this passage teach about money and our attitude toward it?

Why should we avoid friendships with angry people?

Interpret

What does the writer mean by saying, "Bow down your ear" (verse 17)? What imagery is suggested?

Why is it "a pleasant thing" (verse 18) to hear and apply the words of the wise?.

What are the dangers of cosigning loans (verses 26–27)? Do you think these verses represent an absolute prohibition? Why or why not?

How can you "apply your heart" (verse 17) to the Bible writer's knowledge?

When have you gotten into trouble with a loan or payment plan? How might this passage have helped?

How diligent and excellent are you in your business? In what ways could you do better?

Proverbs 22:17–29 Scripture for Memorization/Meditation

Bow down your ear and hear the words of the wise, and apply your heart to my knowledge.
VERSE 17

Verses for Further Memorization/Meditation

- "Give to every man who asks of you. And whoever takes away your goods, do not ask for them back" (Luke 6:30).
- "And if you lend to those from whom you hope to receive, what thanks do you have? For sinners also lend to sinners to receive as much back. But love your enemies, and do good, and lend, hoping for nothing back. And your reward shall be great, and you shall be the children of the Highest. For He is kind to the unthankful and to the evil" (Luke 6:34–35).
- Owe no man anything but to love one another, for he who loves another has fulfilled the law (Romans 13:8).
- Do not be deceived: "Evil company corrupts good manners" (1 Corinthians 15:33).
- And whatever you do, do it heartily, as to the Lord, and not to men, knowing that from the Lord you shall receive the reward of the inheritance, for you serve the Lord Christ (Colossians 3:23–24).

Study 23

PROVERBS 23:17–18, 22–25, 29–35

These "sayings of the wise" have a more direct, urgent, even severe tone than those of Solomon. You may sense more empathy and love in Solomon's admonitions, as a father speaking to his own sons or a king to his nation. Still, these sayings—written by unknown wise men—impart God-inspired lessons.

Even when it seems as if others get away with ungodly behavior, the person who follows God finds true hope, peace, and meaning. The phrase "buy the truth," strange to our twenty-first-century experience, emphasizes the deep value of godly reality. Even adult children should sacrifice to hold on to their wise parents' teaching. When they do, parents have joy in their old age.

Verse 29 begins a series of striking questions, leading to a discussion of drunkenness—a timeless issue. The warning against excessive drinking, which causes disorientation, loss of control, and disregard for wisdom, remains relevant for every generation.

Proverbs 23:17–18, 22–25, 29–35 Outline

(VERSES 17–18)	Do not envy sinners
(VERSES 22–25)	Children should value truth and honor their parents
(VERSES 29–35)	The dangers of indulging in alcohol

Warnings and Instructions, Continued

17Do not let your heart envy sinners, but be in the fear of the
Lord all the day long.
18For surely there is an end, and your hope shall not be
cut off. . . .
22Listen to your father who begot you, and do not despise
your mother when she is old.
23Buy the truth and do not sell it, also wisdom and instruction and understanding.
24The father of the righteous shall greatly rejoice, and he
who fathers a wise child shall have joy from him.
25Your father and your mother shall be glad, and she who
bore you shall rejoice. . . .
29Who has woe? Who has sorrow? Who has contentions?
Who has babbling? Who has wounds without cause? Who has
redness of eyes?
30Those who linger long at the wine, those who go to seek
mixed wine.
31Do not look at the wine when it is red, when it gives its
color in the cup, when it moves itself favorably.
32In the end it bites like a serpent and stings like an adder.
33Your eyes shall see strange women and your heart shall
utter perverse things.
34Yes, you shall be like the one who lies down in the midst
of the sea or like the one who lies on the top of a mast.
35"They have struck me," you shall say, "and I was not sick.
They have beaten me and I did not feel it. When shall I awake?
I will seek it yet again."

Observe

What is the antidote to envying sinners? What are the paybacks of each mindset?

How does a righteous child affect his or her parents?

What are the results of seeking out and lingering over alcohol?

Interpret

Why might these "sayings of the wise" seem more brusque and harsh than Solomon's earlier writings?

What does the lengthy discussion of alcohol and its effects indicate?

Why is the Bible in general, and the Proverbs in particular, so insistent on respect for parents?

Apply

When have you felt a twinge of envy toward sinners? What did you (or should you) do?

How can you honor your parents if they are still alive? What if they have passed on?

What contemporary interests besides wine can become harmful if misused?

Proverbs 23:17–18, 22–25, 29–35 Scripture for Memorization/Meditation

Do not let your heart envy sinners,
but be in the fear of the LORD all the day long.
VERSE 17

Verses for Further Memorization/Meditation

- Honor your father and your mother, that your days may be long on the land that the LORD your God gives you (Exodus 20:12).
- "You shall rise up before the white head and honor the face of the old man and fear your God. I am the LORD" (Leviticus 19:32).
- Do not fret because of evildoers or be envious of the workers of iniquity. For they shall soon be cut down like the grass and wither as the green herb (Psalm 37:1–2).
- And let us not be weary in doing good, for in due season we shall reap, if we do not lose hope (Galatians 6:9).
- And do not be drunk with wine, in which is excess, but be filled with the Spirit (Ephesians 5:18).

Study 24

PROVERBS 24:3–4, 13–22, 30–34

Just as a house becomes a home when it's filled with things that bring comfort, so wisdom makes the soul glad. Its impact is whimsically and beautifully compared to the sweetness of honey—just as honey delights the mouth, so wisdom fills people with hope and joy.

The writer states that the ungodly show foolishness by trying to subdue God's people. Today, believers can rely upon the strength of Jesus—by His Holy Spirit—to endure whatever opposition comes against them. The ungodly do not have this strength and hope, and unless they repent, they will fall into destruction. On the other hand, envying evildoers is not something any believer should do, for the same reason: The path of the unrighteous leads to death.

These verses end with a powerful word picture of wisdom, reminding us that neglect and laziness lead to bad consequences.

PROVERBS 24:3–4, 13–22, 30–34 OUTLINE

(VERSES 3–4)	Building life with wisdom and knowledge
(VERSES 13–14)	Feast on wisdom, and never lose hope
(VERSES 15–16)	The foolishness of opposing the just
(VERSES 17–18)	Never gloat over the fall of the ungodly
(VERSES 19–20)	Godliness brings life; evil leads to death
(VERSES 21–22)	Fear God, respect authority, beware of troublemakers
(VERSES 30–34)	The troublesome consequences of laziness

Warnings and Instructions, Continued

3 Through wisdom a house is built, and by understanding it is established.

4 And by knowledge the chambers shall be filled with all precious and pleasant riches. . . .

13 My son, eat honey, because it is good, and the honeycomb, which is sweet to your taste.

14 So shall the knowledge of wisdom be to your soul; when you have found it, then there shall be a reward, and your hope shall not be cut off.

15 Do not lie in wait, O wicked man, against the dwelling of the righteous; do not plunder his resting place.

16 For a just man falls seven times and rises up again, but the wicked shall fall into evil.

17 Do not rejoice when your enemy falls, and do not let your heart be glad when he stumbles,

18 lest the Lord see it, and it displease Him, and He turn away His wrath from him.

19 Do not fret because of evil men or be envious of the wicked,

20 for there shall be no reward for the evil man; the candle of the wicked shall be put out.

21 My son, fear the Lord and the king, and do not meddle with those who are given to change,

22 for their calamity shall rise suddenly, and who knows the ruin of them both? . . .

30 I went by the field of the slothful and by the vineyard of the man void of understanding.

31 And behold, it was all grown over with thorns, and nettles had covered its face, and its stone wall was broken down.

32 Then I saw and considered it well; I looked at it and received instruction.

[33]Yet a little sleep, a little slumber, a little folding of the
hands to sleep,
[34]so shall your poverty come like one who travels, and
your need like an armed man.

Observe

What qualities are necessary for "building a house," or a good life? What is the result of building in this way?

How do the behaviors and outcomes of the wicked and the righteous differ?

What do laziness and sloth lead to in physical terms? What do they lead to in financial terms?

Interpret

What might "precious and pleasant riches" (verse 4) represent beyond material wealth?

What kind of people could be described as "those who are given to change" (verse 21)? Why would we be warned against meddling with them?

How are "the slothful" related to those "void of understanding" (verse 30)?

Apply

Have you ever wanted to "rejoice" when an enemy fell? Why would the Bible warn against this?

How can you apply the counsel of verses 19–20 to situations in which you see people getting ahead through bad behavior?

How can you keep work and rest in proper balance?

Proverbs 24:3–4, 13–22, 30–34 Scriptures for Memorization/ Meditation

Through wisdom a house is built, and by understanding it is established.
VERSE 3

For a just man falls seven times and rises up again, but the wicked shall fall into evil.
VERSE 16

Verses for Further Memorization/Meditation

- Do not fret because of evildoers or be envious of the workers of iniquity. For they shall soon be cut down like the grass and wither as the green herb (Psalm 37:1–2).
- By much laziness the building decays, and through idleness of the hands the house leaks (Ecclesiastes 10:18).
- Do not avenge yourselves, dearly beloved, but rather give place to wrath, for it is written, "Vengeance is Mine. I will repay," says the Lord (Romans 12:19).
- Let every soul be subject to the higher authorities. For there is no authority but by God, and the authorities that exist are ordained by God (Romans 13:1).
- But if any does not provide for his own, and especially for those of his own house, he has denied the faith and is worse than an unbeliever (1 Timothy 5:8).

Study 25

PROVERBS 25:1–11, 15, 18–19, 21–22

In this section of Proverbs, through the end of chapter 29, we return to the wisdom of Solomon. These sayings were compiled by King Hezekiah's men some two hundred years after Solomon lived. This section covers a wide range of themes, starting with practical wisdom for rulers.

In any dispute, Solomon says it's better to settle privately, since court cases may expose more than a plaintiff cares to make known. Troublemakers, talebearers, and those who plan evil often fall into their own traps.

Solomon discourages revenge on enemies, advising kindness instead. This is a teaching reiterated centuries later by both Jesus and Paul.

PROVERBS 25:1–11, 15, 18–19, 21–22 OUTLINE

(VERSE 1)	Introduction to Solomon's proverbs, as collected by Hezekiah's men
(VERSES 2–7; 15)	A ruler's wisdom and reactions explained
(VERSES 8–10)	Wisdom in handling disputes
(VERSE 11)	The value of well-chosen words
(VERSES 18–19)	False witness against a neighbor is abhorrent
(VERSE 21–22)	The wisdom of showing kindness even toward enemies

Warnings and Instructions, Continued

1These are also proverbs of Solomon, which the men of Hezekiah, king of Judah, copied:

2It is the glory of God to conceal a thing, but the honor of kings is to search out a matter.

3The heaven for height and the earth for depth and the heart of kings is unsearchable.

4Take away the dross from the silver, and there shall come out a vessel for the silversmith.

5Take away the wicked from before the king, and his throne shall be established in righteousness.

6Do not put yourself forth in the presence of the king, and do not stand in the place of great men,

7for it is better that it be said to you, "Come up here," than for you to be put lower in the presence of the prince whom your eyes have seen.

8Do not go out hastily to argue, lest you know not what to do in the end, when your neighbor has put you to shame.

9Debate your case with your neighbor himself, and do not disclose a secret to another,

10lest he who hears it put you to shame, and your shame not turn away.

11A word properly spoken is like apples of gold in pictures of silver. . . .

15By long patience a prince is persuaded, and a soft tongue breaks the bone. . . .

18A man who bears false witness against his neighbor is a club and a sword and a sharp arrow.

19Confidence in an unfaithful man in time of trouble is like a broken tooth and a foot out of joint. . . .

[21]If your enemy is hungry, give him bread to eat, and if he is thirsty, give him water to drink.

[22]For you shall heap coals of fire on his head, and the LORD shall reward you.

Observe

What advice did Solomon, a king, have for dealing with kings (or, in our day, anyone in authority)?

....

....

....

....

What does this passage have to say about pride and humility?

....

....

....

....

How, according to Solomon, should people approach their enemies?

....

....

....

....

Interpret

Why would it be "the glory of God to conceal a thing" (verse 2)? Why is it the "honor of kings" to search them out?

What is the problem with hasty arguments and public debates (verses 8–10)?

How might a man bear "false witness against his neighbor" (verse 18)? Why is that so troublesome?

Apply

How much of an issue is pride in your life? Why?

How much of an issue is conflict with neighbors (or family, or coworkers, or friends) in your life? Why?

What are some practical ways you can honor and serve an enemy?

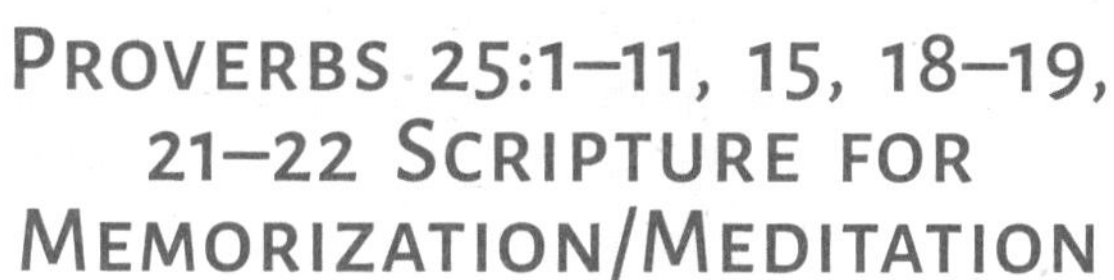

Proverbs 25:1–11, 15, 18–19, 21–22 Scripture for Memorization/Meditation

A word properly spoken is like apples
of gold in pictures of silver.
VERSE 11

Verses for Further Memorization/Meditation

- You shall not bear false witness against your neighbor (Exodus 20:16).
- And he answered, "You shall not strike them. Would you strike those whom you have taken captive with your sword and with your bow? Set bread and water before them, that they may eat and drink and go to their master" (2 Kings 6:22).
- The secret of the LORD is with those who fear Him, and He will show them His covenant (Psalm 25:14).
- Let no corrupt communication proceed out of your mouth, but what is good for the use of edifying, that it may minister grace to the hearers (Ephesians 4:29).
- Walk in wisdom toward those who are without, redeeming the time. Let your speech always be with grace, seasoned with salt, that you may know how you ought to answer every man (Colossians 4:5–6).

Study 26

PROVERBS 27:1–4, 7–10, 17–18, 23–27

The wise King Solomon reminds us not to brag about the future—what we think we will or will not do—because nobody knows what will happen even a moment in advance. Nor should people boast of themselves; if any praise comes our way, let it be the truthful, unprompted words of others. And of course, envy and anger should have no place in the hearts of God's people. These things just lead to harmful conflict.

Friendships, however, are beneficial and powerful, something to cultivate. Good friends challenge and support one another and make each other happy. Just as iron sharpens iron, friends help other friends to become all they can be.

PROVERBS 27:1–4, 7–10, 17–18, 23–27 OUTLINE

(VERSE 1)	Caution against arrogance concerning the future
(VERSE 2)	A warning against self-praise
(VERSES 3–4)	The dangers of anger and envy
(VERSES 7–8)	Dealing with surplus, need, and contentment
(VERSES 9–10; 17)	The importance of friendships
(VERSE 18)	Hard work and loyalty will be rewarded
(VERSES 23–27)	Tend to your God-given responsibilities

Warnings and Instructions, Continued

[1]Do not boast about tomorrow, for you do not know what a day may bring forth.

[2]Let another man praise you, and not your own mouth—a stranger, and not your own lips.

[3]A stone is heavy and the sand weighty, but a fool's wrath is heavier than both of them.

[4]Wrath is cruel and anger is outrageous, but who is able to stand before envy? . . .

[7]The full soul loathes a honeycomb, but to the hungry soul, every bitter thing is sweet.

[8]Like a bird that wanders from her nest, so is a man who wanders from his place.

[9]Ointment and perfume rejoice the heart; so does the sweetness of a man's friend by hearty counsel.

[10]Do not forsake your own friend and your father's friend; do not go to your brother's house in the day of your calamity, for a neighbor who is near is better than a brother far away. . . .

[17]Iron sharpens iron; so a man sharpens the countenance of his friend.

[18]Whoever tends the fig tree shall eat its fruit; so he who waits on his master shall be honored. . . .

[23]Be diligent to know the condition of your flocks, and look well to your herds.

[24]For riches are not forever, and does the crown endure to every generation?

[25]The hay appears and the tender grass shows itself and herbs of the mountains are gathered.

[26]The lambs are for your clothing and the goats are the price of the field.

[27]And you shall have goats' milk enough for your food—
for the food of your household—and for the nourishment of
your maidens.

Observe

What two kinds of boasting are presented in this passage (verses 1–2)? What does Solomon advise?

....

....

....

....

What does Solomon teach about friendship in this passage?

....

....

....

....

What does this passage say about human wrath?

....

....

....

....

....

....

PROVERBS 27:1–4,7–10,17–18,23–27

Interpret

Why would people "boast about tomorrow" (verse 1)? What kinds of things might a day "bring forth"?

How might you "forsake your own friend" (verse 10)? Why would Solomon include "your father's friend" in this advice?

How would you reword verse 8 in contemporary terms? What point is Solomon making there?

Apply

How can you avoid "filling your soul" (verse 7) in ways that make even good things unappealing? Or how can you maintain a spiritual hunger that makes every small gain sweet?

In what specific ways can you "sharpen" your friends (verse 17)?

Taking Solomon's words in verses 23–27 under consideration, what can you do to improve your management of personal resources?

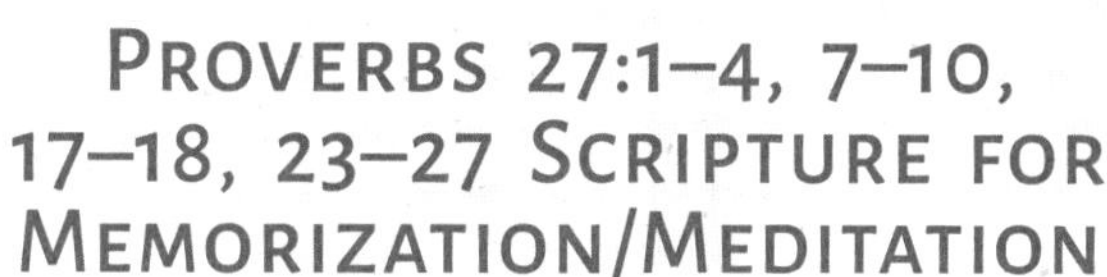

Proverbs 27:1–4, 7–10, 17–18, 23–27 Scripture for Memorization/Meditation

Do not boast about tomorrow, for you do
not know what a day may bring forth.
VERSE 1

Like a bird that wanders from her nest, so
is a man who wanders from his place.
VERSE 8

Verses for Further Memorization/Meditation

- Blessed are those who hunger and thirst after righteousness, for they shall be filled (Matthew 5:6).
- "Take heed that you do not do your deeds of charity before men, to be seen by them. Otherwise you have no reward from your Father who is in heaven" (Matthew 6:1).
- Who, at any time, goes to war at his own expense? Who plants a vineyard and does not eat of its fruit? Or who feeds a flock and does not drink the milk of the flock? (1 Corinthians 9:7).
- Come now, you who say, "Today or tomorrow we will go into such a city and continue there a year and buy and sell and gain a profit," although you do not know what shall happen tomorrow. For what is your life? It is even a vapor, that appears for a little time and then vanishes away. Instead you ought to say, "If the Lord wills, we shall live and do this or that" (James 4:13–15).

Study 27

PROVERBS 28:1–2, 8–18, 23–25

Practical righteousness is a central theme of the Proverbs. In this section, it is seen as beneficial to both individuals and nations. Leaders who govern with integrity and compassion diminish unrest and rebellion, creating stability in their land.

The consequences of unrighteousness—whether dishonoring godly parents, disregarding human life, or living corruptly—are ultimately fatal. Wise people combine prayer and obedience, set a good example, and keep success in its proper perspective. They take responsibility for their own actions and choices, making sure they do right.

PROVERBS 28:1–2, 8–18, 23–25 OUTLINE

(VERSE 1)	Righteousness brings confidence and courage
(VERSE 2)	Righteous leadership leads to peace
(VERSE 8)	There is a cost to ill-gotten wealth
(VERSES 9–14)	Wickedness destroys; righteousness results in good
(VERSES 15–16)	Leaders should govern with integrity and compassion
(VERSES 17–18, 24)	The consequences of selfish and destructive ways
(VERSES 23, 25)	Honest accountability is key to successful living

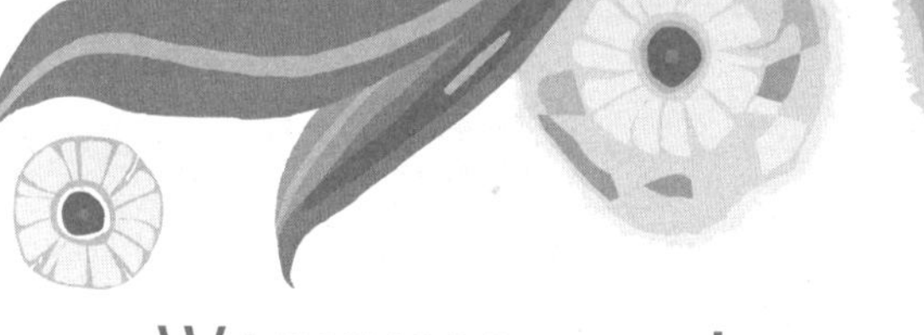

Warnings and Instructions, Continued

1 The wicked flee when no man pursues, but the righteous are bold as a lion.

2 Because of the transgression of a land, many are its princes, but by a man of understanding and knowledge its state shall be prolonged. . . .

8 He who increases his wealth by interest and unjust gain shall gather it for him who will pity the poor.

9 He who turns away his ear from hearing the law, even his prayer shall be an abomination.

10 Whoever causes the righteous to go astray in an evil way, he himself shall fall into his own pit, but the upright shall have good things in possession.

11 The rich man is wise in his own eyes, but the poor who has understanding searches him out.

12 When righteous men rejoice, there is great glory, but when the wicked rise, a man is hidden.

13 He who covers his sins shall not prosper, but whoever confesses and forsakes them shall have mercy.

14 Happy is the man who fears always, but he who hardens his heart shall fall into evil.

15 Like a roaring lion and a ranging bear, so is a wicked ruler over the poor people.

16 The prince who lacks understanding is also a great oppressor, but he who hates covetousness shall prolong his days.

17 A man who does violence to the blood of any person shall flee to the pit; let no man support him.

18 Whoever walks uprightly shall be saved, but he who is perverse in his ways shall fall at once. . . .

23 He who rebukes a man shall find more favor afterward than he who flatters with the tongue.

24 Whoever robs his father or his mother and says, "It is
no transgression," the same is the companion of a destroyer.
25 He who is of a proud heart stirs up strife, but he who
puts his trust in the LORD shall prosper.

Observe

What are the different ways "princes" can lead their nations? What are the results of each?

What negative personal behaviors does Solomon identify as troublesome in this passage?

What positive personal behaviors does Solomon identify as worthwhile?

Interpret

What do you think it means to be "bold as a lion" (verse 1)? How does that compare to the "roaring lion" of verse 15?

How do the sinful behaviors of this passage relate to modern society? What parallels do you see?

Why would rebuking a man lead to "more favor afterward" (verse 23) than flattery?

When have you paid (or required) "interest and unjust gain" (verse 8)? What does Solomon's teaching say to your personal finances?

In what areas of life do you struggle to take responsibility for your actions? How can you better live up to the truths of verses 13–14?

How much of a challenge is pride in your life? How can you put more trust in the Lord and "prosper" (verse 25)?

Proverbs 28:1–2, 8–18, 23–25 Scriptures for Memorization/Meditation

The wicked flee when no man pursues,
but the righteous are bold as a lion.
VERSE 1

Like a roaring lion and a ranging bear,
so is a wicked ruler over the poor people.
VERSE 15

Verses for Further Memorization/Meditation

- "If you lend money to any of My people who are poor by you, you shall not be to him as a usurer. Neither shall you lay usury on him" (Exodus 22:25).
- "You shall not lend on interest to your brother: interest of money, interest of provisions, interest of anything that is lent on interest" (Deuteronomy 23:19).
- Behold, he labors with iniquity and has conceived evil and brought forth falsehood. He made a pit and dug it and has fallen into the ditch that he made (Psalm 7:14–15).
- There is an evil that I have seen under the sun, as an error that proceeds from the ruler: foolishness is set in great dignity, and the rich sit in a lowly place. I have seen servants on horses and princes walking like servants on the earth (Ecclesiastes 10:5–7).

Study 28

PROVERBS 29:9–27

Solomon concludes his sayings in the book of Proverbs with a final affirmation of how authority, correction, and self-discipline shape our lives from childhood onward. He stresses that God's judgment surpasses any human understanding. Ultimately, it is trust in the Lord's ways that matters most in life.

There have always been those who are wise and follow God's ways, and those who are unwise and do not. We today, living in the age of grace, have the benefit of God's Holy Spirit inside to help us live up to the principles that Solomon taught. And we are granted the incredible privilege of approaching God directly through the saving work of Jesus. This is a gift of grace that we should embrace with hearts of thanksgiving and praise.

PROVERBS 29:9–27 OUTLINE

(VERSES 9–10)	Foolishness and conflict
(VERSE 11)	Wisdom demonstrated by restraint
(VERSES 12–13)	Leadership, integrity, and equality
(VERSE 14)	The righteous kingdom (looking forward to Jesus)
(VERSES 15–24)	Summary of themes: children, authority, words, temper, pride
(VERSE 25)	God's judgment overrules human judgment
(VERSE 26)	True justice comes from God, not human rulers
(VERSE 27)	There is active conflict between the righteous and the wicked

Warnings and Instructions, Continued

9If a wise man contends with a foolish man, whether he rage or laugh, there is no rest.

10The bloodthirsty hate the upright, but the just seek his soul.

11A fool utters all his mind, but a wise man keeps it in until afterward.

12If a ruler listens to lies, all his servants are wicked.

13The poor and the deceitful man meet together; the Lord gives light to both their eyes.

14The king who faithfully judges the poor, his throne shall be established forever.

15The rod and rebuke give wisdom, but a child left to himself brings his mother to shame.

16When the wicked are multiplied, transgression increases, but the righteous shall see their fall.

17Correct your son, and he shall give you rest; yes, he shall give delight to your soul.

18Where there is no vision, the people perish, but happy is he who keeps the law.

19A servant will not be corrected by words, for though he understands, he will not answer.

20Do you see a man who is hasty in his words? There is more hope for a fool than for him.

21He who delicately brings up his servant from a child shall have him become his son in the end.

22An angry man stirs up strife, and a furious man abounds in transgression.

23A man's pride shall bring him low, but honor shall uphold the humble in spirit.

24Whoever is partner with a thief hates his own soul; he hears cursing and does not reveal it.

25The fear of man brings a snare, but whoever puts his trust in the LORD shall be safe.
26Many seek the ruler's favor, but every man's judgment comes from the LORD.
27An unjust man is an abomination to the just, and he who is upright in the way is an abomination to the wicked.

Observe

According to this passage, how do foolish and upright people differ?

What does Solomon teach about speech in these verses?

What is clearly stated about "the LORD" in these verses? What is implied?

Interpret

How can wise and foolish people coexist? What should the wise expect when dealing with the foolish?

....

....

....

....

....

....

What parenting advice does Solomon provide in these verses? Why is that such a common theme in the Proverbs?

....

....

....

....

....

....

How could a king's throne be "established forever" (verse 14)? What would this have meant to Solomon personally?

....

....

....

....

....

Whether or not you're a parent with children in the home, how can you use the Proverbs to build into a child's life?

How much interaction should you have with foolish people? How can you help them without being dragged down to their level?

What are some practical ways you can show trust in God rather than worrying about other people's opinions (verse 25)?

Proverbs 29:9–27 Scriptures for Memorization/Meditation

The king who faithfully judges the poor,
his throne shall be established forever.
VERSE 14

The rod and rebuke give wisdom, but a child
left to himself brings his mother to shame.
VERSE 15

The fear of man brings a snare, but whoever
puts his trust in the LORD shall be safe.
VERSE 25

Verses for Further Memorization/Meditation

- Yes, though I walk through the valley of the shadow of death, I will not fear evil, for You are with me. Your rod and Your staff, they comfort me (Psalm 23:4).
- Wait on the LORD and keep His way, and He shall exalt you to inherit the land. When the wicked are cut off, you shall see it (Psalm 37:34).
- He has shown you, O man, what is good. And what does the LORD require of you, but to act justly and to love mercy and to walk humbly with your God? (Micah 6:8).
- Therefore, my beloved brothers, let every man be swift to hear, slow to speak, slow to anger. For the anger of man does not work the righteousness of God (James 1:19–20).

Study 29

PROVERBS 30:1, 3–9, 20–32

Chapter 30 begins the final section of the book of Proverbs, with sayings from little-known figures Agur and Lemuel (chapter 31). These men are only mentioned in these two chapters of Proverbs. Bible scholars speculate that they were contemporaries of either Solomon or Hezekiah.

As a Bible writer, Agur immediately and humbly acknowledges his limitations and lack of wisdom. He quickly asks some inspired rhetorical questions—which we know today find answers in the Lord Jesus Christ.

Agur prays for a life of balanced dependence on God for his daily provision.

PROVERBS 30:1, 3–9, 20–32 OUTLINE

(VERSES 1, 3)	Agur, the author, admits he doesn't know God
(VERSE 4)	But Agur shares inspired words about God and "his son"
(VERSES 5–6)	The Word of God is holy
(VERSES 7–9)	Agur's two requests of God
(VERSE 20)	The human tendency to reject God's law
(VERSES 21–23)	Four examples of social disorder
(VERSES 24–28)	Four examples of wise little creatures
(VERSES 29–31)	Four examples of impressive creatures
(VERSE 32)	A warning against the perils of persistent foolishness

The Words of Agur

1The words of Agur. . . :

3I neither learned wisdom, nor have the knowledge of the holy.

4Who has ascended up into heaven or descended? Who has gathered the wind in His fists? Who has bound the waters in a garment? Who has established all the ends of the earth? What is His name, and what is His Son's name, if you can tell?

5Every word of God is pure; He is a shield to those who put their trust in Him.

6Do not add to His words, lest He rebuke you, and you be found a liar.

7Two things I have requested of You; do not deny me them before I die.

8Remove far from me deception and lies; give me neither poverty nor riches; feed me with food suitable for me,

9lest I be full and deny You and say, "Who is the Lord?" or lest I be poor and steal and take the name of my God in vain. . . .

20Such is the way of an adulterous woman: she eats and wipes her mouth and says, "I have done no wickedness."

21For three things the earth is disturbed, and for four that it cannot bear:

22for a servant when he reigns and a fool when he is filled with food,

23for a hated woman when she is married and a handmaiden who is heir to her mistress.

24There are four things that are little on the earth, but they are exceedingly wise:

25the ants are a people not strong, yet they prepare their food in the summer;

26the rock badgers are but a feeble folk, yet they make their houses in the rocks;

27 the locusts have no king, yet they go forth, all of them
in ranks;
28 the spider takes hold with her hands and is in kings'
palaces.
29 There are three things that go well, yes, four are handsome in walk:
30 a lion, which is strongest among beasts and does not turn
away for any;
31 a greyhound; a male goat also; and a king, against whom
there is no rising up.
32 If you have done foolishly in lifting up yourself, or if you
have thought evil, lay your hand on your mouth.

Observe

Though Agur says he lacks "knowledge of the holy" (verse 3), what insightful things does he ask and say about God in this passage?

What is Agur's two-part prayer request? How does he explain this prayer?

What small creatures are wise in Agur's view? What does he say makes them wise?

Interpret

Where do Agur's rhetorical questions of verse 4 find answers elsewhere in scripture?

How does stealing (verse 9) equate to taking God's name in vain?

Why do you think Agur's teaching of verse 32 follows the examples of four things "handsome in walk" (verses 29–31)?

Apply

How is God "a shield" (verse 5) to you? How well do you put your trust in Him?

How can verses 7–9 inform your perspective on needs versus wants?

How troubled are you by the kind of societal disorder seen in verses 21–23? What can you do about that?

Proverbs 30:1, 3–9, 20–32 Scripture for Memorization/Meditation

Who has ascended up into heaven or descended? Who has gathered the wind in His fists? Who has bound the waters in a garment? Who has established all the ends of the earth? What is His name, and what is His Son's name, if you can tell?
VERSE 4

Verses for Further Memorization/Meditation

- "You shall not add to the word that I command you, nor shall you take away anything from it, that you may keep the commandments of the LORD your God that I command you" (Deuteronomy 4:2).
- "And no man has ascended up to heaven but He who came down from heaven, even the Son of Man who is in heaven" (John 3:13).
- O the depth of the riches both of the wisdom and knowledge of God! How unsearchable are His judgments and His ways past finding out! (Romans 11:33).
- But every man is tempted when he is drawn away by his own lust and enticed. Then when lust has conceived, it brings forth sin. And sin, when it is finished, brings forth death (James 1:14–15).

Study 30

PROVERBS 31:1, 10–31

Proverbs 31 begins with the teachings of King Lemuel's mother (verses 1–9), offering wisdom on leadership, self-control, and justice.

The remaining verses (10–31) form an acrostic poem, where each verse begins with a successive letter of the Hebrew alphabet. In describing a virtuous woman, Lemuel provides both a model of godly living and a personification of wisdom.

Rather than being a checklist for women, this passage illustrates how wisdom is lived out in daily life—through hard work, financial responsibility, generosity, planning, and reverence for God. While it highlights the qualities of a noble wife, its lessons apply to both sexes, married or not.

At base level, the "Proverbs 31 woman" embodies godly character, with the fear of the Lord as the foundation of her wisdom. This truth hearkens back to Proverbs 1, where the book's central theme is introduced: "The fear of the Lord is the beginning of knowledge" (1:7).

Proverbs 31:1, 10–31 Outline

(VERSE 1)	Introducing the wisdom of King Lemuel's mother
(VERSES 10–29)	The many beneficial qualities of the virtuous woman
(VERSE 30)	The fear of the Lord is wisdom
(VERSE 31)	Wisdom's work will be praised

The Words of King Lemuel

1The words of King Lemuel, the prophecy that his mother
taught him. . . .

10Who can find a virtuous woman? For her price is far
above rubies.

11The heart of her husband safely trusts in her, so that he
shall have no need of plunder.

12She will do him good, and not evil, all the days of her life.

13She seeks wool and flax and works willingly with her
hands.

14She is like the merchants' ships; she brings her food
from afar.

15She also rises while it is yet night and gives food to her
household and a portion to her maidens.

16She considers a field and buys it; with the fruit of her
hands, she plants a vineyard.

17She girds her loins with strength and strengthens her
arms.

18She perceives that her business is good; her candle does
not go out by night.

19She lays her hands to the spindle, and her hands hold
the distaff.

20She stretches out her hand to the poor; yes, she reaches
out her hands to the needy.

21She is not afraid of the snow for her household, for all
her household are clothed with scarlet.

22She makes herself coverings of tapestry; her clothing is silk
and purple.

23Her husband is known in the gates, when he sits among
the elders of the land.

24She makes fine linen and sells it and delivers belts to
the merchant.

[25]Strength and honor are her clothing, and she shall rejoice
in time to come.
[26]She opens her mouth with wisdom, and in her tongue
is the law of kindness.
[27]She looks well to the ways of her household and does
not eat the bread of idleness.
[28]Her children rise up and call her blessed; her husband
also, and he praises her.
[29]Many daughters have done virtuously, but you excel
them all.
[30]Favor is deceitful and beauty is vain, but a woman who
fears the LORD, she shall be praised.
[31]Give her of the fruit of her hands, and let her own works
praise her in the gates.

Observe

What physical tasks does a "virtuous woman" perform?

....

....

....

....

According to this passage, who all does the virtuous woman serve?

....

....

....

....

What does King Lemuel say are the rewards for the virtuous woman?

Interpret

How do beauty, worldly favor, and the fear of the Lord interact (verses 29–30)?

Do you think Proverbs 31 expects a virtuous woman to do all of these tasks? Why or why not?

How important is it that the idea of "the fear of the LORD" closes out the Proverbs? Why do you think so?

Apply

How well does verse 26 relate to you? In what ways could you do better in your speech?

How important are favor and beauty (verse 30) to you? How important is fearing the Lord?

How would you like to be remembered in this world? Where does your praise originate?

Proverbs 31:1, 10–31 Scriptures for Memorization/Meditation

Who can find a virtuous woman?
For her price is far above rubies.
VERSE 10

Favor is deceitful and beauty is vain, but a woman
who fears the LORD, she shall be praised.
VERSE 30

Give her of the fruit of her hands, and let
her own works praise her in the gates.
VERSE 31

Verses for Further Memorization/Meditation

- And all the people who were in the gate and the elders said, "We are witnesses. The LORD make the woman who is coming into your house like Rachel and like Leah, two who built the house of Israel, and do worthily in Ephrathah, and be famous in Bethlehem" (Ruth 4:11).
- But those who wait on the LORD shall renew their strength. They shall mount up with wings like eagles, they shall run and not be weary, and they shall walk and not faint (Isaiah 40:31).
- "Let your light so shine before men, that they may see your good works and glorify your Father who is in heaven" (Matthew 5:16).
- Love endures patiently and is kind; love does not envy; love does not boast, is not puffed up, does not behave improperly, does not seek its own, is not easily provoked,

does not think evil, does not rejoice in iniquity, but rejoices in the truth; it bears all things, believes all things, hopes all things, endures all things (1 Corinthians 13:4–7).

- Let your adornment not be the outward adorning of braiding the hair, and of wearing of gold, or of putting on apparel, but let it be the hidden man of the heart, in what is not corruptible, even the ornament of a meek and quiet spirit, which is of great price in the sight of God (1 Peter 3:3–4).